T0169658

BEAT THE HEAT

HOW TO HANDLE ENCOUNTERS WITH LAW ENFORCEMENT

Written by Katya Komisaruk, Attorney at Law
Illustrated by Tim Maloney, Artist at Large

Beat the Heat: How to Handle Encounters with Law Enforcement
by Katya Komisaruk
ISBN 1-902593-55-3

AK Press
674-A 23rd Street
Oakland, CA 94612-1163
USA
(510) 208-1700
www.akpress.org
akpress@akpress.org

AK Press U.K.
PO Box 12766
Edinburgh, EH8 9YE
Scotland
(0131) 555-5165
www.akuk.com
ak@akedin.demon.uk

The addresses above would be delighted to provide you with the latest complete AK catalog, featuring several thousand books, pamphlets, zines, audio products, video products and stylish apparel published and distributed by AK Press. Alternatively, visit our websites for the complete catalog, latest news and updates, events and secure ordering.

Library of Congress Control Number: 2003112984

DEDICATION

This book is dedicated to all the kind women with whom I've done time.

ACKNOWLEDGMENTS

Elektra A., Officer Friendly, Noël Hibberd, and Mike Ruppert reviewed police tactics.

Richard Alejandro and Peter Livingston captured video.

Dustin B., Shaka Cinqué (Albert Woodfox), Ndume Olatushani (Erskine Johnson), Keith Rucker, and Paul Wright discussed incarceration.

Bob Casteel, Leslie Kish, and Jake Scott clarified bail bonds.

Cynthia Collett coached the writer and cleaned up the writing.

Mike Esmailzadeh consulted on nonviolence.

Prof. Chris Gray deconstructed.

Justin Gross submitted to interrogation.

Quiante H., Denisha Q., and Señor X enhanced cartoon dialogues.

Rahula Janowski hooked it up.

Eric Klein laid out the photo novella.

Saba Moeel designed the No Consent to Search notices.

Cloud Morris researched law and finessed forms.

Design Action Collective provided the cover and text design.

Rina Pal and Prof. Samuel Walker addressed systemic discrimination.

Rachael Rakes waited patiently for the manuscript.

Jeff Rector gallantly typeset the pages.

Alison Sexton took the cover photographs, in which Butch Bowen portrayed the cop and Patrukio Mathis portrayed the suspect.

David Solnit offered advice on process.

David Taylor did tech support.

Cris Arguedas, Cindy Cohn, Jim Drew, David Gespass, Vincent Haskell, Douglas Horngrad, Kim Malcheski, Zachary Nightingale, Prof. Frances Olsen, Prof. Bernard Segal, Lee Tien, Norton Tooby, and Ann Winterman—clever, compassionate lawyers all—spent a remarkable amount of time providing suggestions and correcting drafts. (The remaining errors and omissions are, alas, entirely the author's responsibility.)

PURPOSE

In the United States, far too many people are imprisoned, and far too many of the prisoners are low-income people of color. The purpose of this book is to even the playing field, by providing extra legal information to people who can't afford private criminal defense lawyers.

It's particularly important to know your rights at this time, because the behavior of law enforcement toward the public has become increasingly militant and militarized. Law enforcement officers often rationalize their actions as necessary tactics in the wars on drugs or terrorism. Predictably, as these campaigns progress, the primary casualties are people of color, people who are poor, and people who are activists. To make matters worse, recent legislation has given law enforcement greater legal license to pry and intimidate. And these changes in the law signal that the political climate is more accepting of ugly police practices such as infiltration or manipulative interrogation techniques. That's why it's critical to learn how to use the law to protect yourself—before you or the people you care about end up in jail.

PERSPECTIVE

Law enforcement professionals, like lawyers, vary quite a bit in terms of personal integrity. Unfortunately, it's difficult to tell—while you're being arrested—whether the officer you're dealing with is someone you should trust. The officer may be telling you the truth or misleading you. The officer may write down what you say accurately or change it. Or the officer may be honest and careful and still conclude, after talking to you, that you're guilty. You simply won't know whether an officer is really on your side until you read the police report, and by then it's too late. So, people should assume that the officer is not trustworthy, and take the most conservative approach: remaining silent and asking to see their lawyer. This is pretty hard on those cops who just want to sort things out, do their paperwork, and go home. But then, the rights to remain silent and to see a lawyer weren't included in our Constitution to make the legal system more efficient, but rather to make it more fair. And one aspect of fairness is that if you're under arrest and being questioned by a trained professional (a police officer), you're entitled to have a trained professional on *your* side (a defense lawyer), to help you make informed decisions.

Criminal defense lawyers don't urge their clients to avoid taking responsibility for having done wrong. The vast majority of criminal defendants—on the advice of counsel—plead guilty in court. Most of them *are* guilty and sensibly accept a plea bargain instead of going to trial.

Nonetheless, a defendant should plead guilty because he's listening to his conscience or because he recognizes that he's undeniably caught—not because he was manipulated into confessing. But law enforcement officers are trained to mislead suspects whom they're questioning, and it's perfectly legal for police to lie when they're interrogating someone. In particular, officers try to convince people to give up their rights to legal advice before being questioned. Using dirty tricks to get confessions is not only inconsistent with the idea of a just legal system, but also makes it more likely that innocent people will be convicted as well as guilty ones.

Criminal defense lawyers do urge their clients not to answer police questions before talking to a lawyer. But this advice is hard to follow, because it goes against strongly held beliefs. Most people trust the police and want to explain everything. And no one wants to irritate his arresting officer by asking for a lawyer. Even people who are very critical of the police still tend to trust the particular officers who arrest them, and end up submitting to questioning without waiting to see a lawyer. That's why this book gives so many examples of police officers who manipulate suspects into answering questions. It's necessary to focus on the unsavory things police do, in order to convince people they should invoke their rights. And this strategy—remaining silent and asking to see a lawyer—is the safest option even when the officers are honest and just doing their job as they've been trained.

FEEDBACK

The author and illustrator have attempted to be respectful and inclusive of people of assorted gender, race, class, orientation, and physical ability. If you can suggest improvements along these lines, we would be happy to apply them to future editions of this book and to other projects on which we're working.

For those readers who are concerned that this book will help bad people get away with their crimes, we sympathize. Consider, however, that bad things do happen to good people. So it could be handy to know what to say to the police in case they're ever laboring under the misapprehension that you're actually a bad person and therefore deserving of manipulation and mistreatment. On the other hand, you could simply rely on truth as your shield, because in a just legal system that should be perfectly adequate.

DISCLAIMER

What's the difference between a law book and a lawyer? Books are cheaper and it's easier to throw them out of the window when you're fed up with them.[1] However, a book is not a personal consultation with an attorney. You can use this book to learn about the rights that protect you during encounters with law enforcement—but it cannot solve specific legal problems. If you do have a legal difficulty, talk to a lawyer practicing in your area, who can give you proper advice based on the facts of your particular situation and the laws of your particular jurisdiction. If it's a criminal issue, and you can't afford a private lawyer, go see the public defender. And generally speaking, when you're in trouble, the sooner you talk to a lawyer, the better.

Also, remember that the law changes over time, so at least some of the information in this book will go out of date. Check with the publisher or look on the Internet, to make sure you have the most recent edition.

---

1. Secondary Disclaimer: Be aware that *defenestration* (throwing a person or thing out of the window) may result in civil and/or criminal liability, depending on the nature of the object thrown, and its impact on the object on which it lands.

TABLE OF CONTENTS

If you're short on time, read Chapters 1 and 3 (they're the most important ones), then Chapters 4 and 8. Chapter 15 is also very useful.

TABLE OF CONTENTS

If you're short on time, read Chapters 1 and 3 (they're the most important ones), then Chapters 4 and 8. Chapter 15 is also very useful.

INTRODUCTION

HOW THIS BOOK CAN HELP YOU

This book gives you a set of tools to use when law enforcement agents are investigating you or your surroundings. In particular, it teaches you what to say when you're arrested, or when officers want to search you, your car or your home. The information in this book cannot guarantee that you'll win your criminal case in court, but it can definitely increase the odds in your favor.

Any criminal defense lawyer will tell you that cases become significantly harder to win when their clients have answered police questions or consented to searches. Unfortunately, this questioning and searching usually occurs when you're arrested, before you get a chance to consult a lawyer. So you need to know in advance how to use the law to protect yourself.

This book does not teach you how to get yourself "un-arrested" or how to fight your own case in court.[1] Instead, it teaches legal tactics that safeguard an arrested person until the lawyer arrives, in the same way that first aid techniques stabilize an injured person until the ambulance arrives. And while the primary tools—invoking your constitutional rights during questioning or searches—work in all the states and territories of the USA, there are many regional differences in procedure. So be sure to check with a local criminal defense attorney if you have any questions about how best to apply the information in this book.

OPERATING INSTRUCTIONS

The good news is that the methods presented here are simple and are based on using your constitutional rights. The bad news is that the police are legally allowed to manipulate you into giving up your rights, to get you to answer questions and consent to searches. This book will help you learn to recognize law enforcement tricks, so that you won't be taken in if they're used on you.

First, meet our narrator and oracle, Sibyl Rites. She provides legal information and commentary throughout the book, and demonstrates what to say to the police.

Most of the tactics are presented through cartoon stories in which an individual has an unfortunate encounter with law enforcement. In each case, the suspect says or does something wrong, from a criminal defense standpoint. Just as things are looking particularly bleak, Sibyl Rites intervenes, magically transporting the suspect to a place of safety, where they can discuss how to handle the situation correctly. (You'll know they're not in the real world because the cartoons in these parts of the stories have a special border: 𝄢𝄢𝄢𝄢𝄢𝄢.) Sibyl then sends the suspect back in time to the moment when the mistakes began, so that the suspect can do a makeover. Don't skip the endings—you want to imprint in your mind a clear memory of the right way to handle the situation.

---

1. Neither does this volume attempt to describe all the problems with the legal system, nor prescribe how to fix them (which is likely to require a revolutionary change in thinking, at the very least). The ambition here is merely to help keep people from being railroaded, by mapping out some of the pockets of safety that lie scattered through the system (like the alcoves in the walls of the subway tunnel, where you can stand while the train is rushing by).

After each story is an additional explanation of the legal issues.

The most important technique in handling encounters with law enforcement is using your rights to remain silent and to see an attorney. You'll notice that the recommended phrases for invoking your rights are repeated throughout, so that by the time you've read all the stories, you'll have painlessly memorized this response: *I'm going to remain silent. I would like to see a lawyer.* (If that doesn't work for you, there's always tattooing.)

CHAPTER 1

ENCOUNTERS WITH LAW ENFORCEMENT AGENTS

There are three levels of police-initiated encounters. The second two—which are more serious—require a certain level of proof before the police can undertake them.

Encounter	Level of Proof
(1) conversation	none
(2) detention	reasonable suspicion
(3) arrest	probable cause

CONVERSATION

When the police are conducting an investigation, but don't have enough evidence to detain or arrest you, they'll try to get you to chat with them. They may call this a "casual encounter" or a "friendly conversation," etc. If you cooperate, you're likely to give them the very facts they need to arrest you.

If an officer tries to start a conversation with you, find out whether you're free to go. If you are, then you should leave immediately, without saying anything else.

Sometimes, an officer will ask you to come to the police station "to answer a few questions."[1] Don't do it. There's a good chance you'll leave the station in handcuffs. Just tell the officer no. If you're outside, walk away; if you're inside, close the door; if you're on the phone, hang up. Then contact a criminal defense lawyer right away.

DETENTION

Detention is a short period of custody, often occurring while the police are deciding whether or not to arrest you. In order to detain you, the police are supposed to have a reasonable suspicion that you're involved in a crime. This suspicion must be more than a mere hunch, and *the police must be able to put their reasonable suspicion into words.* That's why it's sometimes called an "articulable suspicion." For example, if an officer stops an individual, it would not be enough for the officer to be thinking, "He looked like he was up to something." The officer's thoughts would have to be more specific, such as, "He kept looking in the window of the jewelry store, then walking away, then coming back and peering into the store again. And he wasn't from the neighborhood. He seemed nervous and agitated, so I thought he might be planning a burglary."

Usually, a reasonable suspicion is based on multiple factors, such as: the suspect matches the description of a wanted criminal; the suspect drops an object after seeing the police; the suspect runs away after seeing the police; etc.

Detention is supposed to last only a short time and should not involve changing location, such as going to the local police station.

It may be useful later on, when you're fighting the case in court, to have asked the officer why you're being held. If the officer cannot articulate his suspicion, you may be able to show that your detention was unlawful. Obviously, this tactic works better if you have witnesses who will testify that the officer made an inadequate reply. (Without witnesses, it's just your word against the police officer's, if the officer lies about what he said.)

---

1. "Will you walk into my parlor?" said the spider to the fly. *The Spider and the Fly,* line 1, Howitt, Mary. http://www.maryhowitt.co.uk/poems.htm.

If you do ask why you're being held, memorize the officer's response. Never tell a cop that he doesn't have reasonable suspicion. It won't make the officer let you go, it will only annoy him and remind him to think up a good reason for having detained you, before he writes his report.

During a detention, the police are entitled to pat the outer surface of your clothing, to check for guns, knives or other weapons. If you're detained while driving, the officers can look inside the car for weapons (but not in the trunk). *A detention search is conducted only to ensure that the detainee has no weapon.* While detaining you, once the police have patted you down and haven't felt anything that could be a weapon, they cannot then examine the contents of your pockets. However, they may try to trick you into "voluntarily" allowing them to search further than they're entitled during a detention. The officer will ask you to show him the contents of your pockets, bags, trunk, etc. The request will usually sound like a casual order, especially when the officer uses a commanding tone of voice:

- *Let's see what's in your bag.*

- *Want to pop open the trunk for me?*

- *How about showing me what you've got in your pockets?*

Never give permission to law enforcement officers to search. It's important to state your refusal clearly (rather than just shaking your head), so that the police can't misunderstand.

ARREST

You can be arrested by an officer or a citizen who sees you commit a crime. And even if they didn't see you, the police can arrest you if they have probable cause to believe that you're involved in a felony (or sometimes a misdemeanor, depending on the type of crime and the jurisdiction). The facts adding up to probable cause vary, according to the nature of the case. Say, for example, the police received a call from a store owner that someone matching your description had just spray-painted lots of graffiti all over the front of his store. The police drive to the area and notice you running down the street, about a block from the store, holding a can of spray paint in your hand. Under these circumstances, the police would have probable cause to arrest you. They don't need an arrest warrant as long as they have enough facts for probable cause. Probable cause is more than a reasonable suspicion, but less than the level of proof required to convict you at trial (proof beyond a reasonable doubt).

Once you're under arrest, the police can search your clothes, your body, your bags, your car, etc. In addition, after arresting you, the police can search your "wingspan," the area within your immediate control. Your wingspan could include a whole room, if the room is small enough that you could lunge to any part of it.

A detention frequently turns into an arrest, particularly if you answer the officer's questions. Physically resisting the police will almost always turn a detention into an arrest—even gently touching a police officer can result in charges of assault or battery on an officer. If the police find a weapon or see drugs while detaining you, that's likely to provide the probable cause necessary to arrest you. For instance, the police might detain you to see whether you match the description of a particular crime suspect, and then discover an illegal knife while pat-searching you. Or the police might pull you over when you're driving and detain you to write a ticket, and then spot an open alcoholic beverage container in your car. Once you're under arrest, the police are allowed to search your clothes and body and to go through your bag and/or vehicle.[2]

BASIC RESPONSES TO DETENTION AND ARREST

As soon as you perceive that you're not free to go, say the Magic Words: *I'm going to remain silent. I would like to see a lawyer.* By invoking your rights at the very outset, you make it much harder for the police to trick you into saying things that can be used against you in court.

Of course, remaining silent is hard to do. It's human nature to try to talk your way out of trouble. Nervousness makes people want to talk, too. Naturally, the cops are aware of these tendencies and use them to manipulate you into answering questions. It takes real self-control to exercise your right to remain silent, but it's the best possible thing you can do for yourself, in terms of criminal defense strategy.

The biggest mistake that people make is waiting for the police to prompt them. Since the cops' goal is to get you to provide information, they will carefully avoid giving you a cue that reminds you to be quiet. So as soon as you confirm that you're not free to go (by asking or by trying to leave), say the Magic Words: *I'm going to remain silent. I would like to see a lawyer.*

Do not wait for the police to say "You're under arrest." They do not always say it and they're not required to do so.

Do not wait for the police to read you your rights. They may not bother to do it (and they're not required to read you your rights unless you're under arrest and they want to question you).

Remember that the best defense is a good offense. Say *I'm going to remain silent. I would like to see a lawyer,* early and often. Don't worry if the police make fun of you for saying the Magic Words before they've formally announced that you're under arrest or before they've read you your rights. This teasing is merely another trick, to make you unsure of yourself.

---

2. If you're arrested in your car, the police are allowed to search the passenger compartment, but not the trunk (unless they impound the car).

Training yourself is critical. It's hard to have the right moves in an emergency—like an arrest situation—if you haven't practiced. Soldiers, during their training, are drilled so that they automatically give only their name, rank and serial number when they're being interrogated. You need to develop the same reflexes, because if you've been taken into police custody, you're definitely in enemy hands. Your job is to give only your name and address, then say the Magic Words and stop talking. Because in this situation, the police are not on your side. The officers may just be trying to find a reasonable suspect, or they may dislike your ethnicity or attitude. Whatever the circumstances, once you're not free to go, the smart thing to do is to say: *I'm going to remain silent. I would like to see a lawyer.*

WHY YOU SHOULD REMAIN SILENT AND ASK TO SEE A LAWYER

Of course, you've probably had encounters with the police in which you did explain everything and the police let you go...or at least the consequences (a traffic ticket or a misdemeanor conviction) were no worse than they would have been had you kept silent. And it's true that in some cases, it doesn't matter whether you talk to the police or not. However, on those occasions when your luck or skin-color or clothing or income or politics are against you, talking to the police is more likely to result in going to prison than in going free. And you can't necessarily tell in advance how much trouble you're in. You might think you're being pulled over for making an illegal left turn, when in reality the cops are planning to take you in on felony charges.

Also, even though you may be really clever, you're at a huge disadvantage in trying to maintain control over the conversation when you're being questioned by the police. It's an event that's relatively rare for most of us, and one in which we're generally anxious and distracted. By contrast, this situation is extremely familiar to the police. It's what they're trained to do, and they get more experience at it every day. So even the least talented cop eventually gets pretty good at questioning people. It's arrogant to think that you can win at word games with the police, no matter how good a talker you are. The smart money is on saying only the Magic Words: *I'm going to remain silent. I would like to see a lawyer.* These phrases operate as a verbal condom, adding a critical layer of civil rights protection during interactions with cops.

Many people worry that if they don't cooperate fully with the police and answer all their questions, the officers will increase the charges against them. This is a mistaken assumption. Higher charges are *more* likely if you give the police additional information. And in any case, the offenses that the police choose are mere suggestions. It's the prosecutor who actually decides what crimes to charge against you, based on the information in the police report. So, the less you say, the less material the prosecutor has for thinking up charges.

People also worry that if they remain silent and ask for a lawyer, the police will be annoyed and will take them to jail for sure, instead of releasing them on promise to appear. And it's true that refusing to answer questions and asking for a lawyer can be irritating to the police. But there are two reasons to remain silent and ask for a lawyer anyway:

(1) The police may not have the power to release you. For example, warrants, probation violations, or immigration holds normally require the police to take you to jail. And if you're arrested for a felony, the police definitely can't release you. Yet you won't know, while you're being questioned, whether the police intend to file felony charges or misdemeanor ones. And the police will encourage you to think that you're only facing a misdemeanor, even if they fully intend to charge a felony. That's what happened to Justin in *Use a Pie, Go to Jail,* page 46.

(2) Insisting on your rights may mean that the police choose to keep you in custody, rather than releasing you. But spending a few hours or even a few days in jail (until you can bail out or a get a judge to release you), is better than spending a few years in prison—and that's more likely to happen if you spoil any chance of fighting your case, by answering police questions without talking to your lawyer first.

It's harder in the short run to remain silent and ask for a lawyer, especially when the police seem visibly aggravated with you, but it's much safer in the long run.

People in custody also worry that if they don't answer all questions posed by the police, the officers will treat them more roughly. But being afraid of the police isn't a good reason for failing to use your constitutional rights. It's true that the police sometimes beat people, but it's rarely because the suspect refuses to answer questions. Police violence is principally the result of racism, politics, and just general aggression on the part of the police officer, along with tolerance for such misconduct on the part of the police department—not the result of the victim's behavior. So, if you're dealing with aggressive police officers, you should still protect yourself by respectfully saying, *I'm going to remain silent. I would like to see a lawyer.*

Using a humble tone of voice and facial expression, as well as addressing the officer as "sir" or "ma'am," can be very helpful because police officers tend to be extremely alert to any sign of disrespect (real or imagined). If an officer gets the idea that you're giving him attitude, he'll want to teach you a lesson.[3] Of course, speaking respectfully doesn't come naturally for everyone. Some people speak arrogantly out of habit (and may not be aware of how they sound). Others feel that being humble to a police officer simply costs too much in terms of personal pride or political integrity. And some just can't resist baiting those in authority.[4] It's worth practicing the Magic Words with a friend, or in front of a mirror, so that you develop enough control over your voice and expression to say them properly under stressful circumstances. If you're going to be provocative toward people with guns and clubs, it should be because you choose to do so, not because you can't help it.

WHAT TO WATCH OUT FOR, WHEN YOU REMAIN SILENT AND ASK TO SEE A LAWYER

When you're in custody, once you say *I'm going to remain silent. I would like to see a lawyer,* the police are not allowed to question you—but you actually have to remain silent. You can't talk to the police about anything, not the weather or sports or movies. You can't ask simple questions, like "When do I get my phone call?"[5] Don't make small talk. Don't make jokes. Silent really means silent.

The only exception to remaining silent is giving your name and address. You will have to provide that information if you want to be "released on promise to appear" (the promise to appear is a document, usually a ticket, telling you when to come to court—look at the examples on pages 31–32). Do not give any other information, such as your social security number, the names of family members, employment data, etc. This is important, because one of the most effective police interrogation techniques is to relax the subject by posing safe, normal questions—the kind that come up on countless forms and applications. The cop will seem bored and

---

3. It's important to remember that just because police misconduct is predictable, that doesn't mean you deserve it. Even if you fight or flee, the police are not legally or morally entitled to beat you up. They're supposed to use only as much force as is necessary to restrain you. And they're not supposed to react to verbal provocation. See Chapter 14, Reporting Police Misconduct.

4. My friend David Solnit, in custody at the King County Jail in Washington, was asked to sign a form during booking. All he said was "no," but he said it with so much attitude that six cops promptly piled on him.

5. You should be allowed to make a phone call within a few hours of arrest, usually soon after you arrive at the police station or jail. Normally, you're put in a holding cell that has a telephone in it, though these phones are often rigged so that you can only make collect calls. The authorities are allowed to listen in on your calls from jail, so you must not talk about the incident for which you were arrested or any other illegal activities in which you might have been involved. It's best not even to talk about other people, because then they might be investigated or questioned. The important thing to communicate is that your friends or relatives should get you a lawyer and/or a bail bondsman. If you haven't been given access to a telephone, say: "I would like to call a lawyer." This has the same legal effect as saying, "I would like to see a lawyer," so it doesn't wipe out the protection you get from saying the Magic Words.

business-like, just "getting through all the paperwork." An experienced officer will then move very gradually into questions about the people and incident under investigation, without any pause or change of tone. So don't let them get you on a roll, obediently answering "safe questions." Instead, mentally rehearse exactly what information you're going to give: you're going to say only your name and address, nothing else. If you don't set that limit ahead of time, you'll find yourself answering all sorts of questions, some of which are bound to hurt.

If you've been arrested and you break your silence to give your name and address, immediately follow-up by repeating the Magic Words: *I'm going to remain silent. I would like to see a lawyer.* This restores your constitutional protection, making it illegal for the police to question you further.

There are two common misconceptions when it comes to remaining silent:

Misconception 1: Many people assume that if they say *I'm going to remain silent, I would like to see a lawyer* or "I take the Fifth," then nothing they say afterward can be used against them. That's a ghastly mistake. Saying the Magic Words merely keeps the police from questioning you after arrest, and only as long as you stay silent. If you break the silence by saying anything at all—whether it's a statement or a question—your words can be used against you *and* you'll have destroyed the effect of the Magic Words. You'll have to say them again to be protected from questioning.

Misconception 2: Sometimes people get confused and think that informal conversation is okay, as long they don't "make a statement" or "give a confession." That's dangerously wrong. Anything you say—anything at all—can be used against you, even questions, casual remarks, and jokes. It doesn't matter whether your words are written down or spoken, or whether you're in custody or free to go. And your statements can easily be twisted, taken out of context or misquoted. It's impossible to predict all the things that could go wrong once you start talking. So the only safe course is to remain silent. Here is an example, based on real cases, of people who talked their way into prison:

Example: Sue and Sally were arrested together in a drug case. At the police station, they were kept in separate holding cells, out of earshot of each other. The detective investigating the case questioned them individually about the crime. Neither of them answered these questions. However, Sue chatted with the detective, just making small talk—she told him where she went for dinner the night before, where she was planning to go for vacation, etc. Later on, the detective went to Sally and fooled her into thinking that Sue snitched on her. Sally wouldn't have believed the detective, except that he mixed in the trivial information Sue had given him earlier, and those tidbits of truth made his story very convincing. Once Sally was persuaded that Sue had told on her, Sally angrily insisted it was all Sue's doing. The detective then took Sally's statements to Sue, who was outraged, and promptly ratted on Sally. So in the end, both suspects were suckered into snitching on each other.[6]

When law enforcement officers are questioning you, it's completely legal for them to lie about the evidence and even create false documents in order to fool you into talking! Since you cannot be sure that the officers you're dealing with are telling the truth, the only safe thing to do is to stay silent. As the saying goes, "a fish won't get caught if it keeps its mouth shut."[7]

---

6. For another example of this technique, see *Rat Jacket,* page 63.

7. Attorneys have been giving this particular piece of advice for hundreds of years. Back in 1614, an English lawyer named John Hoskyns (who was, at the time, locked up in the Tower of London for being disruptive) wrote to his young son:

> Sweet Benjamin, since thou art young,
> And hast not yet the use of tongue,
> Make it thy slave, while thou art free;
> Imprison it, lest it do thee.

The Columbia World of Quotations, s.v., "John Hoskyns," http://www.bartleby.com/ (accessed October 16, 2003).

WHY YOU SHOULD REMAIN SILENT AND ASK TO SEE A LAWYER EVEN IF YOU'RE INNOCENT

Remember that you should still say *I'm going to remain silent. I would like to see a lawyer,* even if you haven't done anything wrong. Innocent people are wrongfully convicted of crimes all the time. This happens for a variety of reasons, such as:

- matching the description of a particular crime suspect

- being too near a crime scene (in the wrong place at the wrong time)

- hanging out with people who have been engaging in criminal activity, thus appearing to be their accomplice

- being framed by a lying witness (and sometimes the false witness is a law enforcement officer)

> **Example:** Sam was arrested in connection with a shooting. The arresting officer asked him what happened, and Sam said, "Hey man, it wasn't me. I was there, but I didn't shoot anybody. There was this other guy, I don't know who he was, but he's the one who did the shooting." Well, it turns out that the police had also taken a statement from Willie, an eye witness. Willie didn't get a good look at anyone's face, but he was certain that there were only two men present—the victim and the shooter. So now Sam had a real problem. He'd admitted to being at the scene of the crime and, of course, that "unknown man who did the shooting" was nowhere to be found. Since Willie testified convincingly there was only one other man beside the victim, the jury concluded that the shooter was Sam—since Sam had already admitted that he was present at the incident.

If the legal system worked perfectly, these mistakes would be corrected in court—but the system is flawed. Judges, jurors, lawyers, law enforcement officers, and probation officers all have limitations stemming from racism, classism, sexism, homophobia, plain stupidity, etc.[8] Moreover, in any court case, the parties' resources play a big part in the outcome. (Here in the United States, you get the best justice money can buy.) And money notwithstanding, even the best criminal defense lawyers can't always expose a witness who lies really well.[9]

Don't make the mistake of thinking that the officer who's interviewing you is acting as an impartial judge, sorting out who's naughty and who's nice. The officer is building a case. That's his job. And if you answer questions, you're giving the officer building materials to construct a case against *you*. Contrary to popular opinion, truth is *not* your shield—at least not when you're being questioned and arrested. The time to "explain everything" is when you've got your attorney with you, so you can be sure you won't be misled, misunderstood or misquoted.

---

8. See Appendix A: Suggested Reference Material on Discrimination in the Legal System, page 180.

9. Consider David Harris, who murdered a cop. Harris, a good liar, got Randall Adams convicted and sentenced to death for this crime. The case was the subject of a documentary film by detective-director Errol Morris, who played a critical role in Adams's ultimate release: *The Thin Blue Line,* directed by Errol Morris (1988; Anchor Bay Entertainment, 2000). Unfortunately, for every wrongfully convicted prisoner who is helped by people like Morris or by the network of Innocence Projects, many more unjustly convicted prisoners go unaided.

2

SAFETY TACTICS DURING ARREST

ARMED AND DANGEROUS

BEING ARRESTED IS SCARY. IT'S USUALLY UNEXPECTED, AND SOMETIMES HAPPENS IN A DARK, LONELY PLACE. THE PROCESS IS OFTEN SCARY FOR THE POLICE, TOO. ABRUPT, ANXIOUS BODY LANGUAGE ON THE PART OF THE SUSPECT CAN LEAD TO FATAL MISUNDERSTANDINGS. CONSIDER WHAT HAPPENS TO LUIZ, WHO'S HEADING HOME ONE NIGHT WHEN HE RUNS INTO A COUPLE OF NERVOUS COPS WHO ARE ARMED AND DANGEROUS.

WHAT WAS THAT?

SLAM

OKAY, MAYBE I'M A LITTLE ON EDGE...

HEY, IT'S THE REALITY ON THIS BEAT. LOOK WHAT HAPPENED TO JOHNSON LAST MONTH—AND THAT WAS ON A DAY-SHIFT.

HEY! YOU!

HOLD IT RIGHT THERE!

SAFETY TACTICS

When you have an unexpected encounter with the police or with any other law enforcement agents, you will be safer if you pay attention to your body language.

- Do not make any sudden movements.

- Keep your hands in view and open (so it's clear that you're not holding anything or making a fist). Do not reach into pockets or bags, unless instructed to do so. If the police ask to see identification, tell them where you keep it before you start to get it out.

- Never touch the police or their equipment (vehicles, weapons, radios, flashlights, animals, etc.)

- Breathe deeply, speak slowly, and relax your shoulders and knees. This will reduce the officer's fear that you may be about to attack or run away. Relaxing under these circumstances is harder than it sounds, because our bodies usually produce adrenalin when we're confronted by law enforcement agents. Adrenalin makes us breathe, move, and talk more quickly. So you have to concentrate to slow down, because you're probably going a bit faster than you realize.

- Make eye contact, to indicate sincerity. However, direct eye contact is sometimes perceived as a challenge, depending on gender, size, race, attire, etc. So maintain a respectful facial expression and speak politely. Again, this is harder than it sounds, because most of us feel angry and/or scared when we're dealing with law enforcement agents. If you're perceived as displaying "attitude," the officer will usually try to humble you—then you'll get angrier and so will the officer, a vicious cycle. Your best bet is to control your expression and tone of voice from the outset. Addressing the officer as "sir" or "ma'am" is good, too.

- If you're in a car and an officer indicates that you are to pull over, park as soon as it's safe. Keep both hands on the steering wheel, where the officer can see them. Do not reach into your pocket, bag, glove compartment or visor. Even though the officer will want to see your driver's license and other documents, do not reach for them until the officer asks to see them. When he does tell you to show him your license and papers, say where they are, and confirm that it's okay for you to get them out. For example, "Sir, my license is in my bag here—is it okay if I open it?" or "Sir, the car registration's in the glove box—should I get it out now?" Under no circumstances should you get out of the car—this will be perceived as a threat. If the officer is giving you commands over his loudspeaker, that means he's particularly nervous, so follow the directions carefully and then hold very still.

- If you're walking by police officers, it's best to pass in front, so they don't think someone's creeping up behind them. However, do not walk in front of an officer if doing so would interfere with the officer's access or aim.

DE-ESCALATING EXTREME DANGER

One exception to the rule against talking to the police is the situation in which an officer is extremely frightened, and you feel that a few soothing words may keep him from shooting you. The point is to keep the officer from panicking, not to make *you* feel better by indulging in nervous chatter. This de-escalation involves saying only one or two sentences. After that, you can use non-verbal communication, such as keeping your hands in view, making appropriate eye-contact, breathing slowly, etc.

Note: **Do not focus on this exception and ignore the basic rule. You should only make calming statements when you're facing a cop who's about to panic and shoot. For all other circumstances, you should rely on saying:** *I'm going to remain silent. I would like to see a lawyer.*

What to say to a frightened cop	What *not* to say to a frightened cop
Hey, it's okay, no problem here.	What do you want with me?
It's all right, I'm just passing through.	Fuck you, I ain't done nothing!
I got my hands up.	Don't shoot—I don't have a gun.

It's a natural impulse to yell, "Don't shoot!" or "I don't have a gun!"—but what the police tend to hear is "SHOOT!" and "GUN!" That's because when people are distracted by strong emotions, or by events occurring in the background, they usually focus on the words that are emphasized or that come last in the sentence. Also, it's standard procedure for a cop to yell "gun" when he finds one during a search, in order to alert the other officers. So, referring to shooting or guns in an already tense atmosphere is likely to make things worse.

Once the initial danger is past, it's best to rely on the basic tactics:

- If you're free to go, leave immediately without saying anything else.

- If you're not free to go, say: *I'm going to remain silent. I would like to see a lawyer.*

USING THE RIGHTS TO REMAIN SILENT AND TO SEE A LAWYER

FIVE-FINGER DISCOUNT

LAW ENFORCEMENT AGENTS CAN TRICK YOU INTO GIVING UP YOUR RIGHTS. THAT'S WHY YOU SHOULD SAY: I'M GOING TO REMAIN SILENT, I WOULD LIKE TO SEE A LAWYER, AND THEN KEEP QUIET. BUT WATCH OUT FOR POLICE OR PRIVATE SECURITY WHO GIVE YOU HARMLESS-LOOKING FORMS TO SIGN—THESE DOCUMENTS MAY WELL BE CONFESSIONS OR WAIVERS OF RIGHTS. THAT'S ONE OF THE PLOYS USED AGAINST KAITLIN, WHEN SHE GOES SHOPPING AND DECIDES TO SAVE SOME MONEY WITH THE FIVE FINGER DISCOUNT.

19

THEY *DID* ARREST YOU! AND EVERYTHING YOU SAID TO THEM WILL BE USED AGAINST YOU IN COURT.

LIKE, WHAT'D I SAY THAT WAS SO BAD?

WHAT *DIDN'T* YOU SAY? YOU MADE HALF A DOZEN ADMISSIONS OF GUILT & YOUR STORIES WERE CONTRADICTORY TO BOOT.

THE SMART THING TO DO IS TO INVOKE YOUR CONSTITUTIONAL RIGHTS BY SAYING, I'M GOING TO REMAIN SILENT. I WOULD LIKE TO SEE A LAWYER, AND THEN SHUT UP. ONCE YOU SAY THOSE MAGIC WORDS, YOU'VE INVOKED YOUR RIGHTS UNDER THE 5TH AND 6TH AMENDMENTS TO THE U.S. CONSTITUTION—AND THE POLICE HAVE TO STOP QUESTIONING YOU.

I WAS HOPING THEY'D LET ME GO. I EVEN CRIED.

YEAH, THE CRYING WAS VERY ARTISTIC. I'LL TELL YOU, THEY'VE HEARD IT ALL BEFORE. IF THEY LET A SHOPLIFTER GO, IT'S BECAUSE THE MANAGEMENT HAS A POLICY OF NOT PROSECUTING, OR BECAUSE THE SECURITY GUARD DIDN'T GET ENOUGH EVIDENCE—NOT BECAUSE OF ANYTHING THE SUSPECT SAYS.

SO AGAIN, THE SENSIBLE THING TO DO IS GIVE YOUR NAME AND ADDRESS, AND SAY THE MAGIC WORDS: I'M GOING TO REMAIN SILENT. I WOULD LIKE TO SEE A LAWYER.

BUT IF I HADN'T EXPLAINED, IT WOULD'VE LOOKED LIKE I WAS HIDING SOMETHING.

HOW MANY TIMES DO I HAVE TO SAY IT? THEY ALREADY THOUGHT YOU WERE HIDING SOMETHING—THAT'S WHY THEY GRABBED YOU. THERE'S NOTHING YOU CAN SAY DURING AN ARREST THAT'S LIKELY TO HELP YOU, OTHER THAN THE MAGIC WORDS. WHAT'S MORE, WHEN YOU'RE ON TRIAL, IT'S ILLEGAL FOR THE PROSECUTOR TO MENTION THE FACT THAT YOU REMAINED SILENT AND ASKED FOR AN ATTORNEY WHEN YOU WERE ARRESTED. SO YOU DON'T HAVE TO WORRY ABOUT LOOKING LIKE YOU'RE BEING EVASIVE—YOU CAN'T BE PENALIZED FOR INVOKING YOUR RIGHTS.

NOW, THERE MAY BE A REASONABLE EXPLANATION FOR WHAT YOU WERE DOING, BUT IF SO, IT'LL BE JUST AS EFFECTIVE LATER ON, AFTER YOU'VE GOTTEN AN ATTORNEY.

BUT I DON'T HAVE MONEY FOR AN ATTORNEY!

COME ON, YOU KNOW THE SCRIPT: YOU HAVE THE RIGHT TO REMAIN SILENT. ANYTHING YOU SAY MAY BE USED AGAINST YOU IN A COURT OF LAW. YOU HAVE THE RIGHT TO AN ATTORNEY. IF YOU CANNOT AFFORD AN ATTORNEY, ONE WILL BE PROVIDED FOR YOU BY THE COURT. THAT LAST LINE MEANS THAT THE COURT HAS TO HIRE A LAWYER FOR YOU, IF YOU'RE AT RISK OF BEING SENTENCED TO JAIL.

OKAY, OKAY, SO I SHOULD HAVE SAID, I'M GOING TO REMAIN SILENT. I WOULD LIKE TO SEE A LAWYER. I GET THAT. BUT I STILL DIDN'T HAVE ANY CHOICE ABOUT THE STUFF THEY HAD ME SIGN.

YES, YOU DID. YOU HAD NO OBLIGATION TO SIGN THOSE FORMS.

BUT THAT COP SAID HER FORM WAS JUST TO CONFIRM THAT SHE READ ME MY RIGHTS.

SHE LIED. IT CONFIRMS THAT YOU WAIVED YOUR RIGHTS, MEANING THAT YOU GAVE THEM UP.

AND HERE'S WHAT THE STORE SECURITY OFFICER GAVE YOU TO SIGN—IT'S A CONFESSION TO STEALING.

BUT THAT SECURITY GUY SAID THIS WOULD HELP SHOW THAT I WAS COOPERATIVE.

HE LIED. THIS IS A CONFESSION.

PAYMORE DRUG STORES

1. Kimono Micro-Thins condoms, 12-pack

I hereby acknowledge that on ___ I took for my own use, ___ not intending to pay for ___ above described ___ m the PayMore

SO I SHOULDN'T HAVE SIGNED THOSE THINGS. AND I SHOULD'VE SAID THE MAGIC WORDS. BUT EVEN IF I'D DONE ALL THAT, WOULDN'T I STILL HAVE GOTTEN BUSTED, SINCE THAT RENT-A-COP WAS SPYING ON ME?

OF COURSE. INVOKING YOUR RIGHTS DOESN'T KEEP YOU FROM GETTING CAUGHT WHEN YOU BREAK THE LAW—IT JUST GIVES YOU A FIGHTING CHANCE IN COURT.

AND BY THE WAY, IT'S NO GOOD WAITING FOR THE POLICE TO READ YOUR RIGHTS BEFORE YOU SAY THE MAGIC WORDS, 'CAUSE THEY MAY NOT DO IT. SO DON'T WAIT FOR A CUE. AS SOON AS YOU REALIZE THAT YOU'RE NOT FREE TO GO, YOU SHOULD SAY, I'M GOING TO REMAIN SILENT. I WOULD LIKE TO SEE A LAWYER. NOW, LET'S SEE WHETHER YOU WERE LISTENING...

THE *MIRANDA* RIGHTS

Most of us have watched enough TV to know the *Miranda* rights[1] (also called the *Miranda* warnings) by heart:

- You have the right to remain silent.

- Anything you say may be used against you in a court of law.

- You have the right to an attorney.

- If you cannot afford an attorney, one will be provided for you by the court.

These rights are derived from the U.S. Constitution, so the protection they provide is particularly strong because the Constitution is the ultimate law in every jurisdiction in the United States.[2]

The **right to remain silent** is also called the "privilege against self-incrimination." It means that you cannot be forced to say or write anything that might be used to prove you're guilty of a crime.[3]

The **right to an attorney** means that you're entitled to have a lawyer present to help you during police questioning, line-ups, hearings, etc. Having your lawyer present during interrogation will help you use your right to remain silent.

When **the court appoints an attorney** for you because you can't afford one, that lawyer is usually a public defender or panel attorney (see page 166).

There is no one-and-only correct wording for the *Miranda* warnings—small changes are acceptable. For example, one officer might say "Anything you say *may* be used against you in a court of law," and another police officer might say, "Anything you say *can and will* be used against you in a court of law." Both versions would be considered adequate. However, the officer can't make a change that alters the basic meaning. For example, it would be legally insufficient if an officer said "If you cannot afford an attorney, one *may* be appointed for you by the court." Many police departments instruct their officers to read the *Miranda* rights off a card, so that they're less likely to make a mistake.

If you invoke either of these two rights—the right to remain silent or the right to counsel—the police have to stop questioning you. It's best to invoke these rights together, because that provides both present and future protection from interrogation.

HOW TO INVOKE THE *MIRANDA* RIGHTS

The surest way to invoke your rights is to say the Magic Words: *I'm going to remain silent. I would like to see a lawyer.* These two sentences completely invoke your *Miranda* rights. The reason for memorizing this particular formula is that it's easy to make mistakes.

For example, some people say, "I take the Fifth." That's good, but it doesn't remind you of what you're supposed to be doing: remaining silent and waiting for your lawyer. If you say, "I take the Fifth" and then keep on talking, you cancel the effect. Not only will the police be able to go on speaking to you, but everything you say to them will be used against you in court.

Another error is being too hesitant, as in "I think maybe I'd like to remain silent," or "Do you think I should talk to a lawyer?" Usually, people do this because they're nervous and they don't want to seem impolite. But the police immediately take advantage of this sort of shyness to talk the suspect into answering questions. Justin made this mistake in *Use a Pie, Go to Jail,* page 46.

Finally, some folks give in to the temptation to get fancy, saying things like, "I hereby respectfully invoke my constitutionally-protected rights not to be forced to incriminate myself and to have adequate access to counsel, etc." Such long-winded versions are silly for two reasons. First, you're likely to contradict yourself or leave out something important. Second, it makes you sound

---

1. The *Miranda* rights got their name from a case decided by the U.S. Supreme Court in 1966, in which Ernest Miranda's conviction for rape and kidnapping was overturned because the police questioned him without adequately informing him of his opportunities to remain silent and to obtain legal advice. *Miranda v. Arizona,* 384 U.S. 436 (1966).

2. Occasionally, you'll read a superficial news story claiming, "the *Miranda* protections have been overturned." This is because every so often there's a new high court decision that refines or adapts the use and effect of the *Miranda* warnings. Since most journalists aren't in a position to explain new legal technicalities, they end up oversimplifying the story—and then their editors compound the problem by adding a hysterical title like, "*Miranda* Rights Abolished!" (News is business and sensationalism sells.) So regardless of what the headlines say, don't panic before checking with a lawyer. Besides, the *Miranda* decision only says that, under certain circumstances, the police have to *tell* you about your constitutional rights. Even if the *Miranda* case were overturned, it would just mean that you've got to learn about your rights without input from the police—which, fortunately, you're doing at this very moment.

3. Voice samples and handwriting samples are exceptions to this rule.

stuffy, which annoys the police. It's best to keep it simple: *I'm going to remain silent. I would like to see a lawyer.* This gets the job done, legally speaking, and keeps you from getting the wording wrong or sounding like a wanna-be lawyer.

WHEN THE *MIRANDA* RIGHTS MUST BE READ TO A SUSPECT

Just because the arresting officer didn't read you your rights doesn't mean you can beat your case. Law enforcement agents are only required to read you your rights if both:

(1) you're under arrest, *and*

(2) they want to ask you questions

So if the officers haven't arrested you yet, they can ask you questions without reading you your rights, and your statements will still be used against you in court. For example, during a conversation or a detention (see page 4), the police don't have to read you your rights. As you can guess, a smart cop may try to get all his questions answered before officially arresting the suspect.

Sometimes, officers don't bother to read the *Miranda* rights, because they don't really need to question the suspect. There may be good eye witnesses or surveillance tapes. Or the suspect may just be babbling, as Kaitlin did in *Five Finger Discount,* page 18. After all, why would an officer interrupt with questions if the suspect keeps on making stupid statements without any prompting?

The moral of the story is, don't wait for the police to read you your rights. They may not do it at all, or they may at least wait until you've already made lots of damaging statements.

WHO MUST READ THE *MIRANDA* RIGHTS TO A SUSPECT

Both state and federal law enforcement agents have to read you your rights before they can question you in custody. This includes:

- Police and highway patrol officers
- Sheriffs and U.S. marshals
- FBI, DEA, ATF, and other federal agents
- Park rangers
- Probation and parole officers

The only people likely to have you in custody who don't have to say the *Miranda* warnings are private security staff (security guards, rent-a-cops). These security guards sometimes have fancy uniforms and badges, and carry guns, so it's not always easy to tell them from real police.

You should always invoke your rights, whether or not you're dealing with a real law enforcement agent. It won't hurt you if you say the Magic Words to a private security guard. The worst that can happen is that he'll make fun of you. And you'll at least have reminded yourself of your own best strategy, by saying: *I'm going to remain silent. I would like to see a lawyer.*

HOW OFFICERS TRICK PEOPLE INTO GIVING UP THEIR *MIRANDA* RIGHTS

In 1966, when the U.S. Supreme Court ruled that officers must recite the *Miranda* warnings before questioning arrestees, police across the country were outraged. They were sure that suspects would never again confess or even make a few incriminating statements. However, a year or two later, the police had stopped fussing. They discovered that giving the *Miranda* warnings had very little impact on suspects' behavior. Instead of remaining silent or asking for a lawyer, most suspects whom the police arrested went right ahead and answered questions, completely ignoring the warnings.

Now, decades later, the public seems to feel that the *Miranda* warnings are just part of the arrest ritual, the stage that comes between being handcuffed and being put into the back of the squad car. After all, most officers read the rights in a bored monotone, without any emphasis. So an arrested person is likely to think that the *Miranda* warnings aren't very important (though this is actually the last best chance you have to help yourself). Some officers even refrain from saying, "Do you understand?" at the end, because they don't want people to stop and think. Immediately after reading the warnings, an experienced cop will start asking easy questions about age, marital status, employment, etc. Once suspects have been obediently answering a long string of these questions, they will find it very uncomfortable to stop in the middle, even though the inquiry has shifted from personal background information to pointed questions about the crime under investigation.

When a suspect doesn't immediately start babbling, law enforcement agents have very effective tricks for getting people to start talking. The following are common arguments the police use when they're trying to convince you to answer questions. Notice the false assumption in each one:

What's your problem? We're just trying to clarify what's happened here. And since you say you haven't done anything wrong, what've you got to be afraid of?

FALSE: If you don't answer questions, you must be hiding evidence of guilt.

TRUE: The constitutional right to remain silent would be useless, if exercising it branded you as guilty. That's why, if you invoke your right to remain silent, the police and prosecutor are forbidden to use it against you in court. In fact, during trial, if a prosecutor even implies that you've remained silent out of guilt, your defense attorney can object and call for a mistrial!

When we're done here, I'm going back to the station and write my report. That's what the DA's going to use to decide who to prosecute and for what charges. Right now, all I have for my report is how the other guy said it happened. Of course, you don't have to talk to me, but as far as my report's concerned, this is your last chance to tell your side of the story.

FALSE: If you don't tell your side of the story to the police, you'll lose your chance to talk your way out of being prosecuted.

TRUE: You cannot assume that police officers are neutral, listening to both sides and deciding who's at fault. It's their job to collect potential evidence against people. Prosecutors aren't neutral parties, either. It's their job to prove people guilty. So if you're a suspect and you tell your side of the story to the police and the prosecutor—who, by definition, are not on your side—you will be hurting yourself. The right person in whom to confide is your own defense lawyer. Your lawyer will then help you tell your story to the judge and/or jury, who are the only people whose job it is to listen impartially to you.

Look, you're busted. There's no way you're getting out of this. The best thing you can do for yourself at this point is tell the truth. If you take responsibility now, it'll look a lot better when you get to court.

FALSE: The prosecutor and judge will respect you if you confess immediately upon being arrested.

TRUE: Prosecutors will think you're pretty stupid if you confess to the police, but they'll be happy because it'll be much easier to win the case against you. Judges don't particularly care whether you confess to the police or not, as long as you accept a plea bargain before the case has to go to trial. From a strategic standpoint, admitting guilt is only valuable if you hold it in reserve, so that your lawyer can use it as leverage to cut a deal for you. Confessing before negotiating is like going to buy something you really want, putting all your money on the table and asking, "How much does this cost?"

Above all, do not ask for or accept advice from the officers who have stopped you. They are not there to act as your advocate or judge. Remember that they've been trained to put you at ease, to get you to trust them. Their job is to find, arrest and help convict the suspect. And that suspect is you.

HOW OFFICERS TRICK SUSPECTS WHO HAVE CHILDREN

Police often manipulate suspects who have children into confessing or consenting to searches. The soft approach goes like this:

Hey, I see you're alone here with your kids, and I don't want to make this any harder on you than necessary. I tell you what, if you'll sign this form and answer a few questions, we'll let you make some phone calls right now, to find someone who can come pick up the kids.

The hard approach sounds like:

You know, I could put in a call to Child Protective Services and have a social worker out here within the hour. Do you know how hard it is to get your kids back, once the county takes custody of them?

This is a really tough situation, but it's critical to say the Magic Words, *I'm going to remain silent. I would like to see a lawyer,* no matter how frightened and upset you feel. In the short term, if you refuse to cooperate with the police, they may take your children for a little while—but in the long term, you stand a much better chance of beating the criminal charges and coming home. When you answer questions or consent to searches, you sabotage your chances of winning your case or negotiating a favorable plea bargain—which may result in your going to jail or prison, where you won't be available to your children for a long time.

Remember that as long as there are relatives or a designated guardian who can take custody of your children, the authorities aren't going to put your kids in foster care. The county has no interest in spending resources on caring for anyone's children, if it doesn't have to—and the authorities will be more than happy to turn them over to an appropriate guardian as soon as possible. You can shorten the amount of time your children have to wait to be rescued, if you designate a guardian in advance.[4] To appoint a guardian, it's best to check with a lawyer or law clinic—the procedure varies from jurisdiction to jurisdiction, and you don't want your child's guardian to have to struggle to prove that she's properly authorized. If your children are old enough to understand, have them memorize their guardian's name and telephone number. While waiting to complete the arrangements to designate a legal guardian, you should prepare a letter giving certain adults permission to take care of your child in the event of an emergency. Such a letter is not a substitute for setting up a true guardianship, but it *may* convince the authorities to let the adults you've specified take temporary custody of your child. Sign and date the letter, and leave copies with your child's school, your child's doctor, and each of the adults named in the letter.

ORAL CONFESSIONS AND WRITTEN CONFESSIONS

Some silly people persist in imagining that it doesn't matter what they say to the police, as long as they don't sign anything. Yet the *Miranda* warnings specifically state, "anything you *say* can and will be used against you in a court of law." So this shouldn't be a mystery. However, just to be crystal clear, what you say to cops can be just as harmful as what you write or sign for them.

Here's how the police gather incriminating statements during a typical arrest:

1. At the scene of the arrest, the officer reads the *Miranda* warnings and the suspect fails to invoke his rights. Then the suspect answers the officer's questions. The officer takes notes and later quotes the suspect (accurately or not[5]) in the narrative part of the police report.

2. At the arrest location or at the police station, the suspect is invited to tell his side of the story in a written statement (see examples starting on page 37). Sometimes the suspect himself is asked to write the statement, but usually the suspect talks while the officer does the writing. Officers generally edit as they write: leaving some things out, suggesting particular words, or just inserting their own words. Then the suspect is told to sign the statement. Usually the suspect doesn't bother to read it over, let alone make any corrections; or perhaps the suspect is too frightened or upset to disagree with whatever the officer wrote.

3. At the police station, if it's a serious case, officers will question the suspect again. This interview will normally be audio taped, though sometimes the police use videotape. The officer may also seek a longer, more detailed written statement from the suspect.

Naturally, statements on paper or on tape make it harder to defend the case than oral statements. Yet even brief oral statements can be impossible to deny or explain.

TRAFFIC STOPS

When law enforcement agents stop a car, they may simply be intending to write a speeding ticket—or they may be hoping to find evidence of a greater crime. It can be very hard to tell what the officer's up to, but either way, it's important to maintain careful control of what you're saying.[6]

Even in a routine traffic stop, you can be polite and low-key without babbling. Normally, the first thing an officer says to you, after pulling you over for a vehicular violation is: "Do you know what you just did?" Unless you don't care about getting a ticket, it's silly to say, "Oops, I guess I ran a red light." So don't make damaging statements. Instead, ask: "Should I get out my license, sir?" To offset the fact that you're not answering the officer's question, it's important to convey respect through your tone of voice and facial expression. An officer who believes you're being cocky is likely to indulge in unprofessional conduct.

---

4. It's wise to designate a guardian for your child even if you never expect to get in any trouble with the law, in case you're caught in an accident or other disaster.

5. One of my teenage clients was busted on the street and the cops dragged him over to a wall covered with graffiti. The officer demanded, "Did you write that?" My client carefully replied, "No, I did not." In his police report, the officer wrote: "I asked suspect, 'Did you write this graffiti?' and he responded, 'Yes.'" In court, it was the officer's word against my client's—and we were in juvenile court, so there was only a judge and no jury. Bummer.

6. Also remember to stay in your seat and keep your hands on the steering wheel, where the officer can see them.

Unfortunately, it's perfectly legal for an officer to detain you for a minor vehicular violation, in the hope of turning up evidence of some greater crime. This is called a "pretextual stop."[7] (You can reduce the risk of pretextual stops by driving conservatively and keeping your car "tight": no missing lights, no loose tail pipe, no overdue registration.) These pretextual stops begin as mere traffic tickets, but can become very serious indeed, for example:

> An officer has a hunch that the driver of a certain car has recently purchased illegal drugs, but the officer doesn't have enough proof to detain or arrest the suspect. So the officer decides to make a pretextual stop, and pulls the car over on the basis that the car's left tail-light is broken. The officer checks the driver's license, starts writing a fix-it ticket, and then asks, "Do you have any drugs in your possession?" The driver says, "No, no way." The officer smiles and says, "Fine, then you won't mind if I have a look in the trunk?" The driver replies, "Uh, okay, I guess so." In the trunk, the officer finds a controlled substance.

The driver in this story did two things wrong. First, when the officer asked whether he had drugs, the driver should have said, *I'm going to remain silent. I would like to see a lawyer.* Second, the driver should not have agreed to open the trunk; he should have said, "No, I don't consent to your searching the trunk." Clearly, the officer was already convinced the driver had drugs—he just didn't have enough proof to search or arrest. So the offi-

cer was trying to get the driver to say or do something that would provide probable cause. That's why the driver's best response would have been to refuse to answer questions and refuse to consent to a search—because invoking these rights *cannot* be used by the officer to justify arrest or search.

Passengers in a car that's been pulled over should get the officer to say whether or not they're being detained. When the officer comes up to the car, the passenger should ask, "Am I free to go?" It's possible that the officer might say "Yes," in which case the passenger should get out and walk away. More likely, the officer will say, "No, stay in the car." Making the officer specify this will help the passenger's lawyer argue that the passenger didn't voluntarily submit to investigation. Naturally, the passenger must also say, *I'm going to remain silent. I would like to see a lawyer,* and then stay silent.

PRIVATE SECURITY STAFF

Private security guards, "loss prevention agents," and "asset protection agents," are making a citizen's arrest when they bust you, since they aren't really police. They typically keep you in custody and call the police to come pick you up. They're allowed to restrain you physically, while they wait for the police to arrive. They can grab you, handcuff you, lock you in a room, etc. Like police, security staff are not *supposed* to use more force than is necessary to ensure that you don't escape.

Naturally, private security staff are not required to read you your rights, since they're not really police. However, anything you say to private security can and will be used against you in a court of law. Some businesses instruct their security staff to note, in particular, the "subject's first words at time of detention" (because such statements won't have been well thought out). But all statements, from first to last, made to private security staff are dangerous and likely to be quoted or misquoted in their reports. And it's so very tempting to try to explain everything to the security staff. After all, once in a while this works. Some people have been caught engaging in a minor crime, and then talked and cried their way out of trouble. Obviously, this is more effective while you're still young and cute; and it may work better for girls than for boys.[8] Unfortunately, on the occasions it doesn't work, you'll have sabotaged any hope of a legal defense, because what you've said will certainly be used against you court. That's what happened to Kaitlin in *Five Finger Discount.* Not surprisingly, for those who

---

7. In many instances, pretextual stops have been correlated with racial discrimination, such as detention or arrest for "Driving While Black."

8. One drawback to the winsome approach is that occasionally a corrupt security guard or cop will demand sexual services in exchange for letting you go, which many people find distasteful.

take this gamble, the odds always seem better than they really are. Both cops and casinos win big, betting on the gambler's optimism.

In addition to getting you to make damaging remarks, security staff may also persuade you to give a statement in writing or sign a statement they've prepared for you (see Merchant Confession Forms, page 43).

Most businesses with professional security staff also have clear policies about when and whom to arrest. For example, a store may have rules such as: the security staff must not arrest a suspect unless the agent has had an uninterrupted view of her; or juveniles and first-time shoplifters are let go with a warning. But most businesses that employ security staff have a policy of arresting every valid suspect. And if the suspect runs or fights, or doesn't have i.d., the security staff is virtually certain to arrest him. Security guards nearly always follow the store's policy in deciding whom to arrest—it's just not worth it to the guard to risk getting reprimanded or fired for taking pity on a suspect. Besides, after a few weeks on the job, security staff find that they've heard all the excuses over and over. So when suspects talk to security staff, they only make things worse for themselves.

In a case involving theft, it doesn't matter whether or not the suspect leaves the premises. Once you've picked up someone else's property and taken it to keep, without being entitled to it, that's larceny. Usually, store security staff wait for shoplifters to leave before they grab them, so the suspects can't claim that they were intending to pay for the goods before exiting. But security staff may also arrest shoplifting suspects before they've left the store, since concealing the merchandise indicates that there was no intent to pay.

WHAT TO SIGN: PROMISE TO APPEAR

When you've been arrested, you're likely to be given all sorts of forms to sign. But there's only one kind of document that you can be sure is safe to sign: a "promise to appear" (see page 30). Anything else is probably a trap.

WHAT NOT TO SIGN: WAIVER OF RIGHTS, STATEMENT, PROPERTY RECEIPT, MERCHANT CONFESSION FORM

When law enforcement agents are asking you to sign something, the rule to remember is: don't sign anything other than a promise to appear, without consulting your lawyer. But as further protection, you might as well be familiar with the principal documents used to trick people:

- waiver of rights
- statement
- property receipt
- merchant confession form

These are each discussed in detail below, and you'll have no trouble recognizing them, once you've taken a good look at the samples. However, whether or not you can tell precisely what the officers are trying to get you to sign, you know it can't be any good for you unless it's a promise to appear. On the bright side, there's no need to make a decision in haste. If you've just been arrested and the officers are pressuring you to sign something, ask to telephone your lawyer to check whether you should sign. Of course, the officers are likely to claim that they don't allow phone calls until they've finished all their booking procedures—but don't just give up. Many people, upon being arrested, have persuaded the officers at the station to let them telephone their lawyers in the middle of booking. Some just politely asked to call their lawyer ("May I please telephone my lawyer?") and were allowed to do so. Some had to make the request over and over. And some had to refuse to provide even the most basic information—such as name and address—until the officers let them use the telephone.[9]

If you don't have a lawyer yet, try the public defender's office or a criminal defense lawyer from the yellow pages. Keep your question short and focused:

"Hi, I've just been arrested and the police are telling me to sign a paper that says: _____. Should I sign it?"

When you call a lawyer while you're in custody, the lawyer will doubtless remind you to invoke your rights. She will appreciate hearing that you've already told the police, *I'm going to remain silent. I would like to see a lawyer.*

---

9. Quite a few of my clients have succeeded in calling me during booking, both in state custody and in federal custody. One young man called while being booked by the immigration authorities at the border (he sat down and refused to move until they let him use the phone). Another client, Rahula Janowski, got the police to let her call from the hospital, where she had been taken because of injuries sustained during her arrest. (The police were trying to question her while she waited to be treated for a broken collarbone. She made sure to invoke her rights and call for legal advice before accepting pain medication that would cloud her thinking.)

Once you've consulted with an attorney and carried out his or her advice about what to sign and what information to provide, re-protect yourself from questioning by saying the Magic Words again. After that, make sure you don't say anything else to the officers, because if you break the silence, you will have waived your rights.

PROMISES TO APPEAR

A promise to appear is a document you sign when you're being released from custody, guaranteeing that you'll come to court. It normally specifies the courthouse, date, and time at which you're to appear. The promise to appear may be issued by the police, if you're being released at the scene of the arrest or at the police station. Or, if you were kept in custody, you may be issued one at the courthouse or jail, as part of the process of release on bail or release on your own recognizance. In some places the promise to appear is called a "citation," and when you get one you're "released on citation" or "cited out." In other places, it's called a "summons" or a "ticket." (For more information on procedures for release, see Chapter 13, Getting Out of Jail While Your Case is Pending, page 131.) Promises to appear come in various shapes and colors. Sometime they're printed on full-size paper ($8^1/_2$" × 11"); but they can also be smaller, like traffic tickets.[10]

In some jurisdictions, a promise to appear will clearly indicate that it's not an admission of guilt. For example, citations in California have the following phrases above the signature line: "Without admitting guilt, I promise to appear..." However, in most locations, promises to appear don't have such a useful signal to let you know they're safe to sign. So you have to read carefully, to make sure that the document is nothing but a promise to come to court.

Note that if you fail to appear when you promised, the judge will likely issue a warrant for your arrest (a "bench warrant," page 86).

---

10. Actually, a traffic ticket *is* a notice to appear, except you may be given the option of paying a fine instead of coming to court (unless you want to fight the ticket).

NOTICE TO APPEAR 089754523
CITY AND COUNTY OF METROPOLIS

☐ TRAFFIC ☐ NON TRAFFIC ☒ MISDEMEANOR

DATE MO. DAY YR.	DAY OF WEEK	TIME ISSUED
4 / 1 / 03	TUES	1610

NAME FIRST, MIDDLE, LAST: CHRISTINE SMITH

RESIDENCE ADDRESS: 102 3rd St.

CITY, STATE, ZIP: METROPOLIS, WD 20535

DRIVER'S LICENSE	STATE	DOB MO DAY YR
84612390	WD	5 / 30 / 82

SEX	HEIGHT	WEIGHT	HAIR	EYES	RACE
F	5'6"	130	BLOND	BLUE	WHITE

MISC INFORMATION/EVIDENCE OF FINANCIAL RESPONSIBILITY

VEHICLE LICENSE/VIN STATE — REG MO. / YR — ☐ CV (V C 15210 b)

YEAR	MAKE	MODEL	BODY STYLE	COLOR	☐ HM (V C 353)

REGISTERED OWNER OR LESSEE ☐ (SAME AS ABOVE)

ADDRESS OF OWNER OR LESSEE ☐ (SAME AS ABOVE)

SEE REVERSE SIDE FOR BAIL INFORMATION

YES	NO	VIOLATION CODE - SECTION - DESCRIPTION
☐	☒	PC 123(a) PROSTITUTION
	☐	

☒ BOOKING REQUIRED — ☐ SEAT BELT VC 27315 ( ) — ☐ CHILD SAFETY SEAT VC 27360 ( )

…ATE SPEED — P.F. MAXIMUM SPEED — VEHICLE SPEED LIMIT

APPROXIMATE LOCATION OF VIOLATION(S): 6th AND BROADWAY

INCIDENT NUMBER — JUVENILE NUMBER — INMATE NUMBER

☐ OFFENSE(S) NOT COMMITTED IN MY PRESENCE, CERTIFIED ON INFORMATION AND BELIEF

I DECLARE UNDER PENALTY OF PERJURY THAT THE FOREGOING IS TRUE AND CORRECT. EXECUTED ON THE DATE SHOWN ABOVE AT METROPOLIS, WEST DAKOTA

X John Friendly — BADGE NUMBER 451

ISSUING AGENCY IF NOT METROPOLIS POLICE DEPT

NAME OF ARRESTING OFFICER IF DIFFERENT FROM ABOVE — BADGE NUMBER

WITHOUT ADMITTING GUILT, I PROMISE TO APPEAR AT THE TIME AND PLACE CHECKED BELOW

X Chris Smith

☐ APPEAR OR SUBMIT BAIL AT Hall of Justice, Room 101850 Main St., Metropolis, WD 20500, Within 21 Days

☒ APPEAR AT Hall of Justice 850 Main St., Metropolis — ON MO. DAY YR ▶ 4 / 14 / 03

IN ☐ ROOM 202 9:00 A.M. ☒ ROOM 201 9:00 A.M. ☐ ROOM 575 8:00 A.M. ☐ ____

☐ APPEAR AT Youth Guidance Center 375 Woodruff Ave., Metropolis TIME BETWEEN 1:30 - 4:00 P.M. — ON MO. DAY YR. ▶ / /

ARREST NO: _03-6475_

PFN: _AX5294_

CEN: _22640_

CHARGES: _452.2 Crim. C._

WARRANT/DOCKET NO: _47281_

GOTHAM CITY POLICE DEPARTMENT
PROMISE TO APPEAR
(394.9 CRIM.CODE)

> THIS DOCUMENT IS SAFE TO SIGN, TOO, BECAUSE ALL YOU'RE AGREEING TO IS THAT YOU PROMISE TO APPEAR.

THE PEOPLE OF THE STATE OF EAST CAROLINA VS. _CHRISTOPHER SMITH_
(plaintiff)   (defendant)

In consideration of being released on my own recognizance, I hereby promise to appear in the MUNICIPAL COURT for the Gotham Judicial District, 2233 Waterfront Drive, Gotham City, East Carolina, 20500, telephone (800) 333-4630.

ON: _FRIDAY_ , _8/8/03_ AT _9:00 AM_
     (day)   (date)   (time)

EXECUTED ON: _7/14/03_

SIGNED: _Chris Smith_
                (defendant)

ADDRESS: _320 Southshore Blvd._

CITY/STATE: _Gotham, EC 20535_

OFFICER WILL READ THE ABOVE STATEMENT TO THE DEFENDANT:

BAIL:

Defendant is to be admitted to bail in the sum of $ _300_ dollars, including penalty.

R. Bean
JUDGE, GOTHAM MUNICIPALCOURT

REMARKS:

STAY AWAY FROM PAYMORE DRUGSTORE

J. FRIENDLY   _7/14/03   0125_   _J. Hoover_   _7/14/03   0215_
RELEASING OFICER/AGENCY   DATE/TIME   APPROVING SUPERVISOR   DATE/TIME

WAIVERS OF RIGHTS

Waiving your rights means giving them up—nearly always a mistake. In an encounter with law enforcement, the officers want you to waive your *Miranda* rights: the right to remain silent and the right to have a lawyer present to help you when you're being questioned. If you answer questions after law enforcement officers have recited the *Miranda* warnings to you, you've implicitly waived your rights. Even if you say the Magic Words, *I'm going to remain silent. I would like to see a lawyer,* but then *fail* to remain silent, you've waived your rights.

Although you waive your rights simply by talking, you can always make matters worse by signing a waiver of rights form. Prosecutors like it when the police persuade suspects to waive their rights in writing, because that makes it so hard for criminal defense attorneys to argue successfully that their clients were tricked or forced into making damaging statements. (The forms always say that the suspect understands his rights and knowingly gives them up.)

To get you to fall into this trap, most police departments present you with a waiver form at arrest or during booking. The officer generally pretends that it's just a formality. The waiver may be a separate document, or it may be included in a form for taking your statement (see page 36). Here are some lies the officer may tell, to get you to sign the waiver of rights:

- *Sign here. This confirms that we read you your rights.*
- *This is just an acknowledgment that you understand your rights.*
- *We're not legally allowed to write down your side of the story unless you sign this first.*
- *Look, this is just part of the booking process. Everybody has to sign this form.*
- *You're not going anywhere until you do sign it. You wanna sit here all night? That's fine with me.*

If an officer gives you a waiver of rights form, don't sign it. And don't try altering the form, by crossing words out or writing on it. Just give it back to the officer and say: *I'm going to remain silent. I would like to see a lawyer.*

YOU'RE NOT REQUIRED TO INITIAL ANY OF THESE BOXES OR SIGN AT THE BOTTOM. SO DON'T WRITE ANYTHING AT ALL. THAT WAY YOU CAN'T BE TRICKED INTO GIVING UP ANY RIGHTS.

METROPOLIS POLICE DEPARTMENT
ACKNOWLEDGMENT OF 5TH AMENDMENT ADVISEMENT

I have been advised that I have the following rights according to the 5th Amendment of the U.S. Constitution:	Initials
I have the right to remain silent – that is, to say nothing at all.	
Any statement I make, oral or written, may be used as evidence against me in a trial or in other judicial, non-judicial, or administrative proceedings.	
I have the right to consult with a lawyer.	
I have the right to have a lawyer present during this interview.	
I may request a lawyer at any time during this interview.	
If I decide to answer questions without a lawyer present, I may stop the questioning at any time.	
I may obtain a lawyer of my own choice at no expense to the government.	
If I cannot afford a lawyer and want one, a lawyer will be appointed for me by the court.	
I have read my rights as listed above and I fully understand my rights. No promises, threats, or inducements of any kind have been made to me. No pressure or coercion has been used against me.	
I do not want a lawyer. I am willing to answer questions or make a statement or both, about the offense(s) under investigation.	
I do not want a lawyer and I do not wish to make a statement or answer any questions.	
I want a lawyer. I will not make any statement or answer any questions until I talk to a lawyer.	

SIGNATURE OF SUSPECT	DATE	SIGNATURE OF WITNESS/INTERVIEWER	DATE
[SUSPECT REFUSED TO SIGN]		J. Friendly #667	4/1/03

WAIVER OF RIGHTS

1. I have the right to remain silent.

2. Anything I say can be used against me in a court of l~~~

3. I have the right to an attorney.

4. If I cannot afford an attorney, one will be appointed for m~

REFUSED

I have read and understood the above rights and I hereby waive those rights.

Date:_____   Signed:_____

GOTHAM CITY POLICE DEPT.   10.42.7

STATEMENTS

Law enforcement agents start by trying to trick you into making an oral statement, that is, talking about what happened. If you do make the mistake of speaking to the police, the officer will then want to get your statement in writing.[11] Typically the officer will write down the statement and try to get you to sign it, although sometimes the officer will ask you to write it yourself. If you sign a written statement, regardless of who wrote it, you'll have produced potential evidence that's likely to be extremely damaging.

Most police departments have a specific form for statements, that's part of the complete police report. Many statement forms include a waiver of rights section (giving the *Miranda* warnings), but some don't.

The officer may ask for a written statement at the scene of the arrest, or at the police station, or both. Just say no. Don't write anything at all on the form. And don't sign it.

---

11. Remember that what you say can be just as damaging as what you put in writing. See Oral Confessions and Written Confessions, page 27.

UTILITY REPORT
METROPOLIS POLICE DEPARTMENT

1. CASE NO.
03-08851

2. TYPE OF REPORT

1. ☐ MISCELLANEOUS REPORT

    a. ☐ Incident Report

    b. ☐ Civil Standby

    c. ☐ Hazardous Conditions

    d. ☐ Fire Call

    e. ☐ Ambulance Call

    f. ☐ Assist Outside Agency

    g. ☐ Animal Call

    h. ☐ Other _____

2. ☐ Investigator's Case Summary

3. ☐ Property Report

    a. ☐ Found   b. ☐ Safekeeping

4. ☐ Technician's Report

    a. ☐ Evidence   b. ☐ Photo Log

5. ☐ Supplemental Report

6. ☒ Statement

    a. ☐ Witness   b. ☐ Victim   c. ☒ Suspect

3. DAY – DATE – TIME	4. LOCATION	5. TIME COMPLETED
TUES 4/1/03 1530	6th AND BROADWAY	1555

6. NAME – LAST, FIRST, MIDDLE	7. ADDRESS
SMITH, CHRISTINE	102 3rd ST., METROPOLIS, WD 20535

8. TELEPHONE NO.	9. SEX	10. RACE	11. DOB	12. WITNESSED BY
(202) 456-1111	F	WHT	5/30/82	

13. You have the right to remain silent. Anything you say can be used against you in a court of law. You have the right to talk to a lawyer and have him present with you when you are being questioned. If you cannot afford a lawyer, one will be appointed to represent you before any questions, if you wish one

Do you understand each of these rights I have explained to you?   "YEAH"

Having these rights in mind, do you wish to talk to us/me now?   "NOPE"

14. NARRATIVE

— REFUSED TO GIVE STATEMENT —

> THIS FORM IS MEANT TO BE FILLED OUT BY THE OFFICER, AND THEN SIGNED HERE BY THE SUSPECT. IT INCLUDES A WAIVER OF RIGHTS SECTION (BOX #13, ABOVE).

I HEREBY SWEAR, UNDER PENALTY OF PERJURY, THAT THE FOREGOING IS TRUE AND ACCURATE

_____ (signature)   _____ (date)

15. REPORTING OFFICER	16. NO.	17. APPROVED BY	18. DATE	19. COPIES TO	20. PAGE
J. FRIENDLY	451		4/1/03		1 OF 1

DDA REP ☒ CAR ☐ CITE/REL ☐ NTA ☐

COUNSEL/REL ☐ APPROVAL _____

INCIDENT
☐ ADDITIONAL VICTIMS
☒ ADDITIONAL SUSPECTS
☐ ADDITIONAL RECOVERED LOSS
☐ CHANGE IN REPORT CLASSIFICATION
☐ CHANGE IN REPORT STATUS

GOTHAM CITY POLICE DEPARTMENT

☐ SUPPLEMENTAL

☒ STATEMENT

REPORT # 03-6475

PSN _____

REFER TO # _____

IDN _____

CRIME CODE 604.3 PC

REPORT CLASS THEFT

NAME OF VICTIM/SUSPECT
(S) SMITH

NAME OF PERSON MAKING STATEMENT
SMITH, CHRISTOPHER

RACE W | SEX M | AGE 19 | DOB 1/8/84 | HOME PHONE (202) 456-1111

ADDRESS 320 SOUTHSHORE BLVD, GOTHAM, EC 20535 | BUS NAME/ADDRESS | BUSINESS PHONE

A. ADDITIONAL PERSONS (V/RP/W/S) / VEHICLES B. DETAILS OF OCCURRENCE C. MISC. INFO: STATEMENTS, NEIGHBORHOOD CHECK, CRIMINAL RECORD, ETC. D. PROPERTY
PROPERTY CLASSIFICATION: S-STOLEN R-RECOVERED L-LOST F-FOUND D-DAMAGED

1 (SUSPECT INVOKED RIGHTS) - JF

2

3

4

5

6

7

8

9

10

11

12

13

14

15

16

17

18

19

20

21

22

23

24

25

> THIS SNEAKY STATEMENT FORM DOESN'T EVEN HAVE THE MIRANDA WARNINGS ON IT!

SIGNATURE OF PERSON MAKING STATEMENT THE ABOVE STATEMENT IS TRUE AND ACCURATE:

I HEREBY PLACE THE ABOVE SUSPECT UNDER CITIZENS ARREST ON THE CHARGE(S) INDICATED AND REQUEST A PEACE OFFICER TO TAKE HIM/HER INTO CUSTODY. I WILL APPEAR AS DIRECTED AND SIGN A COMPLAINT AGAINST THE PERSON I HAVE ARRESTED.

CONT
F/U DATE
DBRF BY

COPIES: INV. OFF ☐ _____ DDA ☒ 95 ID# ☐ _____

CII _____ WATCH COM ☐ _____ OTHER ☐ _____

STATUS: PENDING ☒ SUSPENDED ☐ CLEARED ☐
UNFOUNDED ☐ COMPLETED ☐ REFERRED TO DDA

REPORTING OFFICER/# J. FRIENDLY #95 | DATE/TIME COMPLETED 7/14/03 0100 | INITIAL REVIEW | DFU | DPU | FINAL REVIEW

SOUTH VIRGINIA HIGHWAY PATROL
STATEMENT FORM

NAME OF PERSON GIVING STATEMENT: _CHRIS SMITH_

DOB: _5/20/81_   DL#: _N6475089_   DATE: _7/4/03_   TIME: _1830_

ADDRESS: _1382 BAY ST._   CITY: _COAST CITY_   PH#: _(202) 456-1111_

ADMONITION OF RIGHTS (*SUSPECTS ONLY*)

YOU HAVE THE RIGHT TO REMAIN SILENT, ANYTHING YOU SAY CAN AND WILL BE USED AGAINST YOU IN A COURT OF LAW. YOU HAVE THE RIGHT TO TALK WITH AN ATTORNEY AND HAVE AN ATTORNEY PRESENT WITH YOU BEFORE AND DURING QUESTIONING. IF YOU CANNOT AFFORD AN ATTORNEY ONE WILL BE APPOINTED FREE OF CHARGE TO REPRESENT YOU BEFORE AND DURING QUESTIONING IF YOU DESIRE.

SUBJECT INITIALS

DO YOU UNDERSTAND EACH OF THESE RIGHTS I HAVE EXPLAINED TO YOU?   YES ____ NO ____

HAVING THESE RIGHTS IN MIND, DO YOU WISH TO TALK TO US NOW?   YES ____ NO ____

REFUSED

I HAVE READ THE ABOVE STATEMENT AND FIND IT TO BE A TRUE AND CORRECT SUMMARY OF THE EVENTS THAT OCCURRED.

J. FRIENDLY
PERSON TAKING STATEMENT   SIGNATURE OF PERSON GIVING STATEMENT

PROPERTY RECEIPTS

When you're arrested or searched, you're normally given a property receipt listing the items taken away from you. The reason you shouldn't sign a property receipt is that it's an admission that you knowingly possess whatever's on that list—and there may be things on the list that can be used against you in court. For example:

- drugs or drug paraphernalia

- weapons

- large amounts of cash (indicative of illegal business dealings)

- stolen property

- burglary tools (such as a screwdriver)

- vandalism equipment (spray paint or even just a marker)

- address book or other documents with the names of people who may be involved in criminal activities

- keys or documents (such as mail addressed to you) that prove you have ties to a place where criminal activity occurred

- computer or electronic storage media (containing files with incriminating statements or contact information)

Even if you believe that your pockets, bags, backpack and car don't contain anything damaging, you still shouldn't sign a property receipt. Just as it's hard to predict how your words might be used against you, it's equally hard to predict how your possessions might be used to prove guilt. Also, you may have something in your property that you've forgotten about (like the end of a joint in the very bottom of your backpack). And finally, someone else may have put an incriminating item in your bag or car—another suspect (trying to get rid of it) or a corrupt officer (trying to frame you).[12]

The officer trying to get you to sign the property receipt may tell the following lies:

- *If you don't sign it, you won't ever get your stuff back.*

- *If you don't sign it, you won't be released.*

- *Don't worry, it's just part of the procedures here—it doesn't mean anything.*

The police don't need your signature to keep track of the items taken from you—they'll all be labeled with your name and the police report number.[13] And your lawyer can always file a "motion for return of property" to get your things back—that's part of a lawyer's job—you just have to ask. Bear in mind that some items may not be released until the case is concluded, because the prosecutor will claim he needs them for evidence. And some of your property may never be returned anyway. Your belongings can be confiscated if they're used during a crime (like burglary tools) or if they're contraband (like illegal drugs or weapons).[14] Similarly, your money can be seized if the prosecutor claims it was illegally obtained (like drug money). The main thing is to talk to your lawyer, before signing anything that has to do with property.

---

12. A client of mine was arrested one afternoon and taken to the station. Following the arrest, police officers picked up two abandoned guns that were near the scene of the incident, but not in my client's possession. Many hours later, in the middle of the night, my client was being released from jail. The police told him to sign a variety of forms, including a property receipt. At the bottom of the list of items were the two guns. My client said, "These aren't my guns." The officer replied, "Oh, don't worry, it doesn't mean anything. We just had to list them somewhere. Besides, you have to sign this if you ever want to get your stuff back. And anyhow, you won't get released tonight if you don't complete all the paperwork." Now, my client had been wearing some very nice gold jewelry that he didn't want to lose. And he was extremely tired. So he signed the property receipt. Needless to say, it became a real problem in defending the case. There was very little chance of finding the officer who'd lied to him (we didn't know his name or badge number). And even if we could find the officer, it would be hard to prove in court that he told those lies, since we had no witnesses to the conversation.

13. The police don't keep track of your property as a favor to you. They do it in case the prosecutor wants to use it as evidence against you.

14. Also, some property gets lost in the system, through incompetence or greed on the part of law enforcement and correctional officers.

IN AN ARREST FOR PROSTITUTION, HAVING MORE THAN A COUPLE OF CONDOMS IS INCRIMINATING.

METROPOLIS COUNTY SHERIFF'S OFFICE
EVIDENCE/PROPERTY RECORD

Case # 03-08851

Code Section and Description	Date	Deputy	ID #
123 (a) PROSTITUTION	4/1/03	J. DOGG	169

☐ Crime Scene Investigation ☐ Seized by Search Warrant ☐ Property Under Observation ☐ Asset Forfeiture
☒ Arrest ☐ Seized by Consent ☐ Jail Incident ☐ Found Property
☐ Seized by Probation Search ☐ Safekeeping ☐ Civil Attachment ☐ Other ____

Name of ☒ Suspect ☐ Victim ☐ Owner
CHRISTINE SMITH

Address
102 3rd ST., METROPOLIS, WD 20535

Recorder

Finder

☐ Photographed
☐ Processing requested

Item #	Description and Serial #	Source of Item	Clear DOJ	Stored	Bar Code
FM1	BLACK HANDBAG	(S) SMITH — ON PERSON			
FM2	BLACK WALLET	"			
FM3	BLACK PLANNER/ADDRESS BK	"			
FM4	BLACK NOKIA CELL PHONE	"			
FM5	11 DUREX GOLD COIN CONDOMS	"			
FM6	9 ASTROGLIDE SINGLES PKTS	"			
FM7	RED NEGLIGEE	"			
FM8	BOX OF BABY WIPES	"			
FM9	$680 (IN WALLET)	"			

Under penalty of perjury the person signing to receive the property declares that s/he is the legal owner and/or possessor of the above described property.

(SUSPECT REFUSED)
Signature of Owner/Possessor

____
Date

White – *Evidence*　　　　**Yellow** – *Report*　　　　**Pink** – *Receipt*

GOTHAM CITY POLICE DEPARTMENT

PROPERTY/CLOTHING RECORD

> THIS BOY HAS BEEN ARRESTED FOR VANDALISM. HE CERTAINLY WAS SILLY TO CARRY AROUND THOSE PHOTOS OF HIMSELF AND HIS GRAFFITI.

DATE OF ARREST	PD CONTROL NUMBER	HANGER NUMBER	GC NUMBER
7/12/03	03-6475	1603	47281

LAST NAME	FIRST NAME AND MIDDLE INITIAL	TELEPHONE NUMBER	
SMITH	CHRISTOPHER	(202) 456-1111	1/8/04

PROPERTY INVENTORY

CASH $7.88 TO BOOKS	BELT	BRACELET
EARRINGS	GLASSES	HAT
KEYS 2 W/KEYCHAIN	KNIFE	LIGHTER
NECKLACE	PAGER	PURSE
RINGS	WALLET 1 BLACK VINYL	WATCH 1 BLACK

MISCELLANEOUS PROPERTY		BULK PROPERTY
1 CAN BLACK SPRAY PAINT 1 CAN RED SPRAY PAINT .5 SPRAY TIP 2 BLACK SHARPIE MARKERS	1 MINI PHOTO ALBUM W/24 PHOTOS OF (6) SMITH AND/OR GRAFFITI SITES W/TAG "LUV-N-RAJ"	

PRISONER SIGNATURE	OFFICER ITEMIZING PROPERTY	BADGE NUMBER	DATE	TIME
X —REFUSED—	FRIENDLY	95	7/12	2315
PERSON RECEIVING PROPERTY	OFFICER RETURNING PROPERTY	BADGE NUMBER	DATE	

CLOTHING INVENTORY

DRESS/SKIRT	FOOTWEAR	JACKET
CONDITION: POOR FAIR GOOD	CONDITION: POOR FAIR GOOD	CONDITION: POOR FAIR GOOD
(SHIRT)/BLOUSE	(SWEATER)	(TROUSERS)
RED/BLACK T-SHIRT	BLACK HOODIE SWEATSHIRT	BLACK
CONDITION: POOR FAIR GOOD	CONDITION: POOR FAIR GOOD	CONDITION: POOR FAIR GOOD
(UNDERGARMENTS) INCLUDING (SOCKS)	MISCELLANEOUS CLOTHING	
CONDITION: POOR FAIR GOOD		

PRISONER SIGNATURE	OFFICER SEARCHING CLOTHING	BADGE NUMBER	DATE	TIME
X —REFUSED—	FRIENDLY	95	7/12/03	2330
	OFFICER ITEMIZING CLOTHING	BADGE NUMBER	DATE	TIME
	"	"	"	"
PERSON RECEIVING CLOTHING	OFFICER RELEASING CLOTHING	BADGE NUMBER	DATE	TIME

NAME SMITH, CHRISTOPHER
JAIL NUMBER AX5295
HANGER NUMBER 1603   BIN NUMBER

MERCHANT CONFESSION FORMS

In stores with well-organized security, the staff normally tries to get shoplifters to sign confession forms.[15] These forms vary in style and, of course, you won't see the word "confession" anywhere on the document. Often, the really deadly part is in the fine print.

Security staff may try to persuade you to sign the confession form by pretending that it's harmless, saying things like:

- *Oh, this? It's just the standard paperwork. We have to do this for every incident. It's no big deal. Sign here.*

- *This document will help you later on, because it shows that you co-operated and didn't try to run away or struggle.*

- *If you sign this, it will make you look better in court, because it'll prove to the judge that you took responsibility for your actions.*

- *Don't worry, you're not going to jail or anything. You'll just get probation and have to stay out of the store from now on. Of course, it's your choice. You can refuse to sign and see what happens…*

These merchant confession forms are used in two ways:

1. The store security staff gives the confession form to the police, who will pass it along to the local prosecutor, to use as evidence against you in a criminal case.

2. The store security staff gives the confession form to the store's lawyers, to use as evidence against you in a civil case (usually a lawsuit to make you pay the store money).

Merchants nearly always give their confession forms to the police, for use in criminal prosecution. They can file civil suits instead of or in addition to this, but they rarely do so, because it's not worth the money they'd have to pay an attorney to do the legal work. However, merchants sometimes send threatening letters to shoplifters, saying that if the person doesn't pay some large sum of money, the store will sue him. This is likely to be an empty threat. Don't respond to a demand letter from a merchant without first consulting a lawyer. (On the other hand, if you receive a letter from the prosecutor's office or from the court, that's serious. You should immediately contact a criminal defense lawyer.)

---

15. Of course, even if you don't sign a merchant confession form, you'll still be in trouble if you talk to the store's security staff. The security agent will write down whatever you say (accurately or not) in his report, and that will definitely be used against you in court.

Shorts Drug Stores, Inc.

SECURITY INCIDENT
STATEMENT OF FACTS

STORE CASE # 4930

Date 3/15/03   Time 6:35 a.m. (p.m.)

Name _____
        (First)   (Middle)   (Last)

refused to answer

Address _____
        (Number)   (Street)

_____
        (City)   (State)   (Zip)

Home Phone _____   SSN _____

On this date I entered Shorts #354 Gotham City , where, without making
                              (location name and number)

payment or arranging credit therefore, I removed and carried from the premises of Shorts,
without any authorization, the following described property:

Merchandise	Value
Condoms	$ 7.47

THIS IS THE CONFESSION TO THEFT.

HERE THE SUSPECT IS INVITED TO MAKE ADDITIONAL DAMAGING STATEMENTS.

My reason for committing this wrong was (refused to answer)
_____
_____
_____

I make this statement because it is the truth. No promise of any kind has been made to me,
and no threats, coercion, force, violence or hopes of reward have been made or used against
me to induce me to make this voluntary statement.

I have also been made aware that I may be contacted later by Shorts' General Office
regarding this case.

W. Wackenhut   (refused to sign)
Witness to Signature   Signature

W. Wackenhut - Loss Prevention Agent
(Print Name and Position)

PayMore
Drug Stores

Date __7/12/03__	Store # __88__	Adult __X__
Time Stopped __3:05__	Region __EC12__	Juvenile _____
Time Released __4:20__		Accomplice ____

Name: Last	First	Middle	DOB		Age
Address			How Long?		
DL# or ID#		SS#		Phone ( )	
Height	Weight		Hair	Eyes	Sex
Purchase Amount		Receipt #		Clothing Description	
Register #		Amount Tendered		Change Received	
Cash: $ 7.88		Checks: Yes (No)		Credit/Debit Card: Yes (No)	
Charge(s) PETTY THEFT		Responding Person/Case #		Disposition	
Father		Address		Phone ( )	
Mother		Address		Phone ( )	

Description	Price	Quantity	Description	Price
RED SHARPIE MARKER	1.59			
BLACK SHARPIE MARKER	1.59			
SPRAY TIPS	NA			
			Total $	

I, _____, do hereby acknowledge that I was in the above store on the above date between the hours of _____ and _____, and while there appropriated to my own use, without paying for nor intending to pay for, the above described items. In signing this statement and surrendering the aforementioned items, I do so voluntarily and of my own free will, without threats or promises of any kind having been made to me, and with the understanding that I fully release the above mentioned store or company and all its agents and representatives individually and personally from all types of civil liability. I have read the above statement and declare that it is true in every aspect.

T. PINKERTON
Witness _____

Signature [REFUSED]
Address _____
_____

HERE'S THE KIND OF FINE PRINT YOUR MOTHER ALWAYS WARNED YOU ABOUT. THE FIRST PART IS THE SUSPECT'S VOLUNTARY CONFESSION TO THEFT. IN THE SECOND PART, THE SUSPECT PROMISES NOT TO SUE IF THE STORE PERSONNEL HURT HIM IN ANY WAY.

45

USE A PIE, GO TO JAIL

THE FOLLOWING MATERIAL IS NOT FICTIONAL. IT'S THE TRANSCRIPT OF A RECORDED POLICE INTERROGATION, OBTAINED IN PREPARATION FOR THE TRIAL OF THE "CHERRY PIE THREE" (WHO WERE PROSECUTED FOR THROWING PIES AT THE MAYOR OF SAN FRANCISCO). THE SUBJECT OF THIS INTERVIEW, JUSTIN GROSS, KINDLY CONSENTED TO PUBLISHING THIS MATERIAL.

THE YEAR THAT THE MAYOR OF SAN FRANCISCO RENEWED THE GOLD LEAF ON THE DOME OF CITY HALL, A RECORD NUMBER OF HOMELESS PEOPLE DIED OF EXPOSURE ON THE STREETS BELOW. SO THE BIOTIC BAKING BRIGADE DONNED THEIR APRONS AND EMBARKED ON A MISSION TO SERVE THE MAYOR HIS JUST DESSERTS—A TART REJOINDER TO THE UPPER CRUST.

JUSTIN GROSS (A.K.A. AGENT MINCED MEAT OF THE BIOTIC BAKING BRIGADE) WAS TAKEN INTO CUSTODY FOLLOWING THE PIE-THROWING. UNFORTUNATELY, JUSTIN DID NOT KNOW THE MAGIC WORDS: I'M GOING TO REMAIN SILENT. I WOULD LIKE TO SEE A LAWYER. AS YOU'LL SEE IN THIS TRANSCRIPT OF HIS INTERROGATION, IT TAKES HIM SEVERAL TRIES TO STOP THE QUESTIONING—AND SOME OF HIS SEEMINGLY HARMLESS ANSWERS CAN INDEED BE USED AGAINST HIM IN A COURT OF LAW.

TODAY IS A GOOD DAY TO PIE.

LISTEN TO THE AUDIO RECORDING OF THIS ACTUAL INTERROGATION, TO GET THE FULL EFFECT OF THE POLICE INSPECTOR'S KIND AND REASSURING TONE OF VOICE! IT'S ON THE JUST CAUSE LAW COLLECTIVE WEBSITE: HTTP://WWW.LAWCOLLECTIVE.ORG/.

Inspector Lundgren: All right, today's date is November the 7th, 1998. The time is approximately 11:08 hours. This is regarding case 98-1432362. I'm Inspector Lundgren, Special Investigations Division and, sir, could you state your name for me, please?

Justin: My name is Justin Gross.

Insp. Lundgren: Okay, Justin, and your date of birth, please?

Justin: October 15, 1971.

THIS WOULD'VE BEEN A GOOD TIME TO SAY THE MAGIC WORDS.

Insp. Lundgren: Okay. Justin, there was an incident this morning in which I was notified and that's why I've come in, and I'm trying to assess what's happened here. This incident occurred around the Civic Center area. Prior to discussing that particular incident with you, I'd like to advise you of your constitutional rights, since technically you're in a police station, okay? You have the right to remain silent; anything you say can and will be used against you in a court of law. You have the right to have an attorney present prior to any questioning, if you wish, and if you cannot afford to hire an attorney one will be appointed to represent you. Justin, do you understand each of those rights as I've explained them to you?

Justin: Mmhmm.

DANGER, DANGER! THIS WOULD'VE BEEN A REALLY GOOD TIME TO SAY THE MAGIC WORDS.

Insp. Lundgren: Okay, and having those rights in mind, would you like to give me your side of the story, or your perspective on what might have happened this morning?

Justin: All I would like...I'd just like to say that we're completely nonviolent activists.

"YOUR SIDE OF THE STORY..." THERE'S A CLASSIC INTERROGATION LINE FOR YOU.

THIS KIND OF STATEMENT MAY BE USEFUL IN THE COURTROOM, BUT NOT IN THE INTERROGATION ROOM.

Insp. Lundgren: Okay. All right, in view of that, was there an intent to inflict great bodily injury upon the Mayor, Mayor Willie Brown of San Francisco?

Justin: No.

Insp. Lundgren: Okay.

Justin: I think that's all I'd like to say.

Insp. Lundgren: That's all you'd like to say?

Justin: For now. Before talking to a lawyer...

JUSTIN'S MUSHY HERE, HE HASN'T FIRMLY SAID, I'M GOING TO REMAIN SILENT. SO LUNDGREN PROBES A LITTLE.

47

Insp. Lundgren: Okay, so, at this point you're indicating to me that you'd like to talk to an attorney?

Justin: Well, if we're going to be held...

Insp. Lundgren: Okay, well, and that's certainly your right, there's no question about that. Whether you're going to be held or not, that's what we're here for, is to try to evaluate the situation. The more information we have to evaluate the situation, the better decision we can make, obviously. So, it's certainly within your rights to ask for an attorney, so if that's what you're doing in effect, then we'll terminate this interview.

Justin: Yeah, it's just, I don't want to, you know, say anything that could come back on me, you know what I mean?

Insp. Lundgren: Certainly, that's, again, that's within your rights.

Justin: But, I would just, you know, once again, I, you know, absolutely no harm was intended, you know. We're nonviolent activists.

LUNDGREN IS TRYING TO TELL WHETHER JUSTIN IS INVOKING HIS RIGHTS. IF ONLY JUSTIN HAD SAID "YES" AND REMAINED SILENT, THAT WOULD'VE ENDED THE QUESTIONING.

ANOTHER CLASSIC LINE. LUNDGREN IS DANGLING THE BAIT THAT HE MIGHT JUST RELEASE JUSTIN WITH A CITATION (A PROMISE TO APPEAR) AND LET HIM GO HOME, RATHER THAN TAKING HIM TO JAIL— IF ONLY JUSTIN WILL ANSWER THE QUESTIONS.

THAT'S ALMOST ALWAYS A FALSE HOPE. IN THIS CASE, WE KNOW FOR SURE THAT LUNDGREN IS LYING. THE POLICE HERE HAVE THE POWER TO ISSUE CITATIONS IN MISDEMEANOR CASES, BUT NOT IN FELONY CASES.

AND REMEMBER WHAT LUNDGREN SAID EARLIER ABOUT "INFLICT GREAT BODILY INJURY UPON THE MAYOR?" THAT'S A FELONY. JUSTIN WILL BE KEPT IN JAIL ON $5,000 BAIL.

IF ONLY JUSTIN HAD LEFT WELL ENOUGH ALONE. SAYING "NO HARM WAS INTENDED" CAN BE TAKEN AS AN ADMISSION THAT THE MAYOR REALLY WAS HARMED BY JUSTIN'S ACTIONS.

Insp. Lundgren: Okay. All right, and when you say "activist," would you like to expound on that? Again, I don't want to lead you into a discussion which ... Okay, you're shaking your head "no," is that correct? All right, would you like to terminate this interview?

INSP. LUNDGREN IS SO POLITE AND CAREFUL NOT TO PRESSURE ANYONE. THE POLICE DEPARTMENT'S SENSITIVITY TRAINING REALLY PAID OFF.

Justin: Please.

Insp. Lundgren: Okay. All right, the time is now approximately 11:09 hours.

PIE FLIES WHEN YOU'RE HAVING FUN.

VERDICT AND SENTENCE IN THE CHERRY PIE THREE CASE

During the course of their nine-hour deliberation, the jury sent out several notes with questions for the judge. One message read: "Can we consider this an act of comedy, rather than an act of battery?" And the judge said "no." Later on, the jurors wrote: "Can we follow the spirit of the law, rather than the letter of the law?" And the judge said "no."

So the jury found the Cherry Pie Three guilty. And the judge sentenced them to six months in jail.[16]

Too bad the jurors didn't know that they *did* have the power to declare the defendants not guilty. "Jury nullification" is the traditional right of every juror to acquit a defendant in a criminal trial, regardless of the strength of the evidence against him. This safety valve in our legal system allows you to follow your conscience in those cases where mechanically applying the law would produce an unjust verdict.

To learn more about the history and politics of jury nullification, see James J. Duane, *Jury Nullification: The Top Secret Constitutional Right,* 22 Litigation 6 (Summer 1996); also posted on the Just Cause Law Collective website: http://www.lawcollective.org/.

---

16. Yet while Justin and his comrades languished behind bars, the Biotic Baking Brigade seized the moral pie ground. The BBB called upon dissident chefs around the world to participate in Operation Dessert Storm…and from many nations, *entartistes* and *flanistas* responded, lobbing their culinary comments at the pompous and powerful, in a global pastry uprising. In the words of Noël Godin, renowned Belgian flan-flinger and the author of *Cream and Punishment*: "There are a thousand forms of subversion, all of them interesting. But few, in my opinion, can equal the convenience and immediacy of the cream pie."

IT'S NOT ENOUGH JUST TO SAY THE MAGIC WORDS: I'M GOING TO REMAIN SILENT. I WOULD LIKE TO SEE A LAWYER. YOU THEN HAVE TO KEEP FROM BREAKING YOUR SILENCE, DESPITE THE CLEVER TRICKS LAW ENFORCEMENT AGENTS EMPLOY TO LURE YOU INTO TALKING. ONE OF THESE TECHNIQUES IS USED ON PHILLIP, WHO'S JUST BEEN ARRESTED WITH A ...

POCKETFUL OF FELONY

I DIDN'T DO NOTHIN'! WHY YOU MESSIN' WITH ME, MAN?

YOU ARE UNDER ARREST FOR POSSESSION OF A CONTROLLED SUBSTANCE WITH INTENT TO DISTRIBUTE. YOU HAVE THE RIGHT TO REMAIN SILENT. ANYTHING YOU SAY MAY BE USED AGAINST YOU IN A COURT OF LAW.

YOU HAVE THE RIGHT TO AN ATTORNEY. IF YOU CANNOT AFFORD AN ATTORNEY, ONE WILL BE APPOINTED FOR YOU BY THE COURT. NOW THEN. WHAT'S YOUR NAME?

PHILLIP WONG. I'M GOING TO REMAIN SILENT. I WOULD LIKE TO SEE A LAWYER.

THAT'S YOUR CHOICE. LET'S GET GOING.

HEY, YOU HEAR WHAT SGT. PETERS DID WITH THAT KID WE BUSTED LAST WEEK—WHAT'S HIS NAME, YOU KNOW WHO I MEAN, THE LITTLE GUY WITH THE BIG ATTITUDE?

I REMEMBER THAT KID. ANNOYING LITTLE SHIT. WHAT'D THE SARGE DO WITH HIM?

WELL, YOU KNOW THAT TANK WHERE THEY HAVE ALL THE GANG-BANGERS FROM 5TH ST.? THE CELL THEY CALL THE "BUTCHER BLOCK?"

SARGE DIDN'T PUT HIM IN THERE, DID HE? BOY, OH, BOY...LAMBS TO THE SLAUGHTER. BET THAT KID'S ATTITUDE CHANGED IN A HURRY. WONDER IF THEY LEFT HIM ANY TEETH...

COME TO THINK OF IT, THIS KID WE GOT HERE NOW ISN'T SO BIG EITHER. FOR HIS SAKE, I HOPE HE KNOWS ONE OF THOSE MARTIAL ARTS. OTHERWISE, HE'S JUST GONNA BE FRESH MEAT. HE'LL GET PUNKED FOR SURE.

YEP, DOWN AT THE YOUTH AUTHORITY THEY GOT GUYS WHO HAVEN'T BEEN OUTSIDE IN YEARS, GUYS WHO HAVEN'T HAD A WOMAN IN A MIGHTY LONG TIME. I'D SAY AS SOON AS HE GETS THERE, IT'S GONNA BE "BEND OVER BOYFRIEND."

THAT WAS AT THE BEGINNING, RIGHT? AND THEN WHAT HAPPENED?

WELL, THE POLICE DIDN'T ASK ME ANY QUESTIONS AFTER I INVOKED MY RIGHTS. BUT EVEN THOUGH THEY WEREN'T TALKING TO ME, THEY WERE KIND OF TALKING AT ME. YOU KNOW WHAT I MEAN? IT MESSED WITH MY HEAD. CAN THEY DO THAT?

THEY JUST DID.

NO, I MEAN, WAS THAT LEGAL? SAYING STUFF TO EACH OTHER, THAT WAS AIMED AT ME? AFTER I SAID I WANTED A LAWYER AND ALL? THAT'S LIKE SOME KIND OF MIND-GAME. IT'S NOT FAIR.

IT MAY NOT BE FAIR, BUT IT'S LEGAL.

ONCE YOU'VE SAID THE MAGIC WORDS, YOU HAVE TO BE QUIET—AND STAY QUIET. IF YOU START UP A CONVERSATION WITH THE POLICE, YOU GIVE UP YOUR RIGHTS. ONCE YOU START TALKING TO THEM, THEY CAN ASK YOU ANYTHING THEY WANT.

YOU MEAN, WHEN I SAID, "WHAT'S GONNA HAPPEN TO ME?" THAT CANCELED OUT THE MAGIC WORDS? I LOST MY RIGHTS TO NOT ANSWER QUESTIONS AND TO HAVE A LAWYER? FOR GOOD?

NO, NOT FOR GOOD. THERE'S AN EASY WAY TO FIX MATTERS IF YOU FORGET TO REMAIN SILENT. CAN YOU GUESS WHAT IT IS?

UH, SAY THE MAGIC WORDS AGAIN?

THAT'S RIGHT. IT'S KIND OF LIKE FLIPPING A SWITCH. WHEN YOU SAY, I'M GOING TO REMAIN SILENT. I WOULD LIKE TO SEE A LAWYER YOU'VE TURNED YOUR RIGHTS ON—THE POLICE CAN'T QUESTION YOU.

BUT IF YOU START UP A CONVERSATION WITH THE POLICE, EVEN JUST ONE QUESTION, YOU'VE TURNED YOUR RIGHTS OFF AGAIN, AND THEY CAN INTERROGATE YOU.

HOWEVER, IF YOU REALIZE YOU'VE MADE THAT MISTAKE, YOU CAN FIX IT BY SAYING THE MAGIC WORDS AGAIN. THIS TURNS YOUR RIGHTS BACK ON.

BUT WHAT IF YOU'VE ALREADY SAID TOO MUCH?

IT'S NEVER TOO LATE TO INVOKE YOUR RIGHTS BY SAYING THE MAGIC WORDS. YOU MAY NOT HAVE SAID AS MUCH AS YOU THINK. AND IN ANY CASE, GOING ON ANSWERING QUESTIONS CAN ONLY MAKE THINGS WORSE.

Once you say the Magic Words: *I'm going to remain silent. I would like to see a lawyer,* the police must stop asking you questions. However, they sometimes try to provoke you into breaking your silence, by talking to each other about all the horrible, terrible things that could happen to you in jail. That's what the officers did to Phillip in *Pocketful of Felony.* When the police are playing this game, they'll make scary predictions about how you'll be beaten up and/or raped by large, vicious prisoners of a different race.[17] (Some officers lead a rich fantasy life.) Just remain silent.

If you've been arrested and realize that you accidentally said something to an officer, don't panic. As soon as you remember that you're supposed to be remaining silent, repeat the Magic Words: *I'm going to remain silent. I would like to see a lawyer.* Just because you've answered some questions doesn't mean that all is lost. You may not have said anything that bad yet. But if you go on talking, you're bound to say damaging things eventually. Besides, the officers are likely to start tape recording you or trying to get you to sign a statement. Stopping can't hurt, and it may help. Don't fall for the old "the cat's out of the bag, so you might as well tell us everything" routine.

---

17. Although this does happen, it's rather unlikely. See Appendix C: Advice for Those Going to Jail for the First Time, page 183.

4

RESISTING INTERROGATION

It's unlawful for the police to beat you into confessing;[1] however, it's perfectly legal for them to sucker you into it. That's why interrogation doesn't usually involve bright lights and rubber hoses—more often than not, the officer sounds sympathetic or at least business-like. And that can leave you even more vulnerable to manipulation, because when you feel relieved that the officer isn't being really scary, you tend to let your guard down. Besides, it's truly difficult to overcome the natural urge to talk one's way out of trouble. That's why it makes so much sense to train yourself to say *I'm going to remain silent. I would like to see a lawyer,* under any circumstances. It's got to become a reflex you can rely on, the same way you know that you'd automatically start swimming if you fell into deep water, even if you were scared and disoriented.

COMMON INTERROGATION LINES

 You're not a suspect. We're simply investigating here. Just help us understand what happened and then you can go.

If you answer questions, you're likely to *become* a suspect, if you aren't really one already.

 What are you afraid of? If you haven't done anything wrong, then you shouldn't have any problem answering my questions.[2]

What you should be afraid of is being lured into answering questions. You don't have anything to prove. Remember, in court you're "innocent until proven guilty"—and the thing most likely to prove guilt is an unplanned statement made when you're arrested. If the police are thinking of arresting you, answering their questions will make them more determined to do it, not less so.

 Look, if you don't answer my questions, I won't have any choice but to take you to jail. This is your chance to tell your side of the story.

This is the commonest trick of all! The police consistently pretend that they're considering letting you go, when they've already made up their minds to take you to jail. Remember, the time to tell your side of the story is when you're in court and have your lawyer helping you—not when you're alone with a cop who's busy building a case against you. See how a real police inspector uses this technique during an actual interrogation, in *Use a Pie, Go to Jail,* page 46.

Your friends have all cooperated and we let them go home. You're the only one left. Do you WANT to stay in jail?

 The police can lie about where your friends are and what they've said. Take a look at *Rat Jacket,* page 63. Don't trust information given to you by the cops. Make sure to verify your facts through a lawyer or your friends and family.

 I'm tired of screwing around. If you don't answer my questions, you're going to be charged with obstruction.

Well, you know this is garbage, because the Constitution guarantees you the right to remain silent—so refusing to answer questions can't be against the law. But some cops will still threaten you with "resisting an officer" or "obstruction of justice," just to see whether you'll fall for it.

---

1. The Fifth Amendment to the U.S. Constitution says that no one "shall be compelled in any criminal case to be a witness against himself."

2. This is not the time to launch into a political discussion of how the legal system is malfunctioning and can't be trusted to protect the innocent. Don't let yourself be drawn into any kind of conversation at all. Besides, this "what're you afraid of" business is like a 12-year-old's dare ("If you're so tough, why don't you try getting across the tracks before that train comes?" or "You don't even know the first thing about how to drive—let's see you take your Mom's car around the block.").

Come on, I'm not asking you to sign anything. We're just talking. And you can stop any time you want to.[3]

Remember, anything you *say* can be used against you in a court of law. You don't have to sign anything to make it a real confession—the police will just quote you (and they may be taping you, too). The time to stop is before you ever begin—even a little time spent answering questions can completely screw up your case.

Look, we've got all the evidence we need to convict you, so you might as well confess.

Yeah, right. If the police really had all the evidence they needed, they wouldn't waste time talking to you. The only reason they're questioning you is because they *don't* have enough proof, and they're hoping you'll be kind enough to give it to them.

Basically, the case against you is really strong. It's not a question of WHETHER you're going to jail—it's a question of what you're going to jail for. This is your last chance to get the right information to the DA before he decides on the charges.

This is not the time to give more information to the DA (the prosecutor). You can do that later, once you've got a lawyer helping you. After all, the DA can change the charges any time up to trial, and usually does—reducing or dismissing them as part of a plea bargain. But your lawyer can get you a better deal if you don't give away all your bargaining power by confessing to the arresting officers.

You know, there's only one person who can help you right now, and that's you. I can listen, but you've got to do the talking. This thing is going to eat at you; it's going to weigh you down for the rest of your life, if you don't get it off your conscience. Things look pretty bad right now, and they are. But this is where you have to start from. You've got to get this stuff out now, so you can move forward. If you could talk to the victim right now, what would you want to say to him?

 Confession may be good for the soul, but not when it's to the police. Talk about your feelings with a spiritual advisor such as a minister, priest, rabbi or imam, or with a licensed counselor such as a psychiatrist, psychologist, or social worker (but not a probation officer). They have the professional training to help you, and more important, they're prohibited by law from testifying about what you confide to them. Cops, on the other hand, will gladly testify about what you've "gotten off your chest."

You got a choice here. Either you answer my questions, or you're going to jail. And I'd hate to see a nice white boy like you get punked by a bunch of nigs.[4]

– or –

You can talk to me now, or you can go to jail. And let me tell you something, there's women in that jail who haven't been outside in months, women who haven't been with a man for a real long time. How'd you like to be raped by a bunch of lesbians?[5]

Cops use this kind of race-baiting and queer-bashing pretty frequently to scare white people who haven't been to jail before. And the cops aren't particularly subtle about it. Don't let some bigot with a badge put his trash into *your* head.

TV and movies make rape-in-jail scenarios look more frequent than they really are. Most people in jail are there for drug or property crimes, not crimes of violence (much less sexual violence). If you behave reasonably, other prisoners really aren't likely to give you a hard time. See Appendix C: Advice for Those Going to Jail for the First Time, page 183.

3. This is a lot like: "Don't worry, we can stop whenever you want to. Besides, you can't get pregnant the first time."
4. Said to Mike Esmailzadeh by a New Orleans cop.
5. Said to Katya Komisaruk by a U.C. Berkeley cop.

GENERAL INTERROGATION TECHNIQUES

You know the police are really trying to manipulate you when they offer a legal defense or moral justification for what you're accused of doing, or imply that what happened was due to an accident or to circumstances beyond your control.[6] In applying this tactic, the interrogator frequently offers the suspect two choices, for example: a believable explanation or an unbelievable one; an honorable excuse or a dishonorable one. Of course, both choices are still damaging admissions—it's just that one *sounds* better than the other. Imagine the following lines said by a sympathetic, understanding police officer in a warm, reassuring tone of voice:

Legal Defense

- *I understand what you're saying...he threatened you, and essentially you were acting in self-defense.*

- *Okay, we've got you for possession of marijuana. But what isn't clear to me is: were you just out to get stoned, or were you maybe using it for medical purposes?*

Moral Justification

- *What I'm wondering is whether you needed that money so you could take care of your kids and get them decent food and clothes and all—or did you just do it because you wanted drugs or new Nikes or whatever?*

- *Well, that's a perfectly normal reaction. When a man finds out that his wife is sleeping with another guy, he's going to want to go out and do something about it.*

Accident or Circumstances Beyond Control

- *Now, I wasn't there, so I don't know. Only you know what really happened. But I'm thinking that when two people get into it, when there's an argument, stuff can happen that nobody ever intended. I mean, you could've just been shoving each other around, and he could've fallen and hit his head by accident—just plain bad luck.*

- *Obviously there's a difference between being an active participant and being a bystander. It's one thing to be actually involved in selling the drugs, and it's another thing to just be in the house when some other guys are doing a deal there. But the way things look, you could be either one. And the only way we're going to be able to figure out what your real role was, is if you talk to us.*

Another common aspect of Reid interrogation is **minimization/maximization,** contrasting the worst case scenario with the best possible outcome.

- *You know, there's a lot of different ways this case could be charged. Anywhere from first-degree murder—that gets you life without parole—all the way down to involuntary manslaughter, for which people typically get probation. What we're doing right now is trying to understand what really happened, so we can make a decision which way to go...*

Often the police will even say, "Look, I'm not making any promises..." and then *imply* that confessing will result in a better outcome in court: lesser charges, a more favorable sentence, etc. This is a lie. The police are not authorized to offer leniency in exchange for a confession. Only the prosecutor or judge can make a plea bargain.[7]

All law enforcement officers are trained to question suspects. Very few civilians have any practice in spotting or withstanding the interrogation techniques police use against them. It's pretty stupid to play such lousy odds when your liberty's at stake.

---

6. John Reid codified these tactics, referring to them as the "Nine Steps of Interrogation." Reid and his partner Fred Inbau spent decades writing about and teaching interrogation techniques, and business is still booming at http://reid.com/. In U.S. police academies, their books have been the most popular texts on this subject. Their work is full of sample scripts, generally involving a hapless suspect named Joe: "Joe, if this whole thing was your idea, that tells me that you have a criminal mind. But if you were just talked into doing this against your better judgment, that would be important to include in my report. You were just talked into it, weren't you?" For examples of how such techniques get innocent people to confess to crimes, take a look at the work of Richard Ofshe, at http://sociology.berkeley.edu/faculty/ofshe/.

7. There's a difference between confessing and snitching. A law enforcement officer can't offer you a deal in return for a confession, but he can make a snitch deal. See Informants, page 79.

GOOD COP, BAD COP

RAMÓN FINDS OUT THE HARD WAY THAT THE GAME IS RIGGED, WHEN HE COMES UP AGAINST A TEAM OF OFFICERS IN THE GOOD COP, BAD COP ROUTINE.

I WANNA PHONE CALL. I BEEN HERE FOR THREE HOURS, MAN. I GOT A RIGHT TO A PHONE CALL. HOW COME I AIN'T GOT MY PHONE CALL YET?

HOW COME? HOW COME? BECAUSE YOU'RE A MOTHERFUCKING ASSHOLE! LET ME TELL YOU SOMETHING, SHITHEAD. I DON'T LIKE YOU. I DON'T LIKE YOUR FUCKING ATTITUDE.

GODDAMMIT, YOU'RE GONNA FUCKING LOOK AT ME WHEN I'M TALKING TO YOU. YOU GOT THAT? YOU GOT THAT, ASSHOLE?

OKAY, MOTHERFUCKER, YOU DON'T WANNA GIVE ME A SINGLE STRAIGHT ANSWER TO SINGLE FUCKING QUESTION I ASK. OKAY, FINE. I'M GONNA MAKE IT MY BUSINESS TO SEE THAT YOU GET PUT AWAY ON THIS CASE. I'M GONNA MAKE SURE YOU GET SOME REAL TIME.

NOW, TAKE IT EASY, SARGE. JUST GIVE HIM A CHANCE...

GIVE HIM A CHANCE? THAT PUNK'S HAD ALL THE FUCKING CHANCES HE'S GONNA GET! I'VE HAD IT WITH THAT FUCKHEAD. I WANT HIS ASS OFF THE STREETS PERMANENTLY. AND I'M GONNA HAVE A LITTLE TALK WITH THE D.A. ABOUT IT. THEN WE'LL SEE IF HE GETS ANY FUCKING PHONECALLS.

HEY, RAMÓN, YOU GOTTA WATCH IT WITH SGT. PETERS. HE GOES OUT OF HIS WAY TO GET PEOPLE SOMETIMES. YOU DON'T WANT HIM GOING AFTER YOU—HE CAN MAKE SOME SERIOUS TROUBLE. LOOK, WHY DON'T I GO TRY AND CALM HIM DOWN? I'LL TELL HIM YOU DIDN'T UNDERSTAND BEFORE, AND YOU'RE READY TO ANSWER QUESTIONS NOW, OKAY?

It's initially surprising that the Good Cop, Bad Cop routine works so well, since it's generally so obvious. You've seen it in hundreds of TV shows and movies, and most people consider it a cliché. Yet law enforcement officers use it in every city, every day…because it works nearly every time. And a big reason it works so well is that when you've just been arrested, you're extremely vulnerable. You're thinking of all the horrible things that are likely to happen: going to jail, disappointing your loved ones, being publicly disgraced, losing your job, failing school, etc. On top of that, if you've been in custody all day or all night, you'll be suffering from fatigue and hunger, and perhaps other physical stresses. So, psychologically, you're a sitting duck. And even though you know, intellectually, that the good cop is just trying to manipulate you, you cannot help having hope and trust in the one person in this awful situation who seems to be on your side. It's a tough problem, but there is a solution. The answer is to train your mind, so that you say *I'm going to remain silent. I would like to see a lawyer,* no matter how upset you're feeling or how kind the officer seems. "Don't just practice until you can get it right, practice until you can't get it wrong."[8]

Of course, sometimes the cops aren't pretending. The bad cop may, in fact, have lost his temper and be yelling at you for real. Or the good cop may truly want to help you, and may think that your answering questions will somehow benefit you. But whether or not the cops are sincere, *your* strategy remains the same. You should still say: *I'm going to remain silent. I would like to see a lawyer.* Because if the bad cop really does want to make trouble for you, your giving a statement will make it easy for him. And the good cop, in urging you to answer questions, is giving you bad advice. Some officers honestly think that if a suspect makes a statement, it will be helpful. But it doesn't work that way in court. Prosecutors can almost always find *something* in suspects' statements that can be used against them. That's why, when you do tell your side of the story, you should do it with the help of your defense attorney—so that your words can't be twisted or misquoted.

If you're arrested with friends, make an agreement that no one will make statements to the police until everyone's been able to talk to a lawyer and decide calmly what to do. Be aware of the paranoia that tends to set in after people have been separated. When a person's isolated, it's much easier for the police to lie and convince him that his friends have snitched. So make sure everyone understands: *nobody talks, everybody walks.*

Warning: Do not have a strategy discussion in the backseat of a police car! If you've been arrested with someone else, and the cops lock the two of you in their car and walk away, you can bet dollars to donuts that they're recording your conversation. So if you're in this situation, just remind the other person that the smart thing to do is to say: *I'm going to remain silent. I would like to see a lawyer.* And leave any further discussion until later.

When you're in jail, don't talk to your cell-mates about what happened to you or who was with you—because you really don't want them testifying at your trial or sentencing hearing. Don't even talk about mutual acquaintances. Stick to safe topics such as movies, music, sports, etc. You'll make it a lot harder for anyone to snitch on you, if you don't snitch on yourself.

---

8. Harold A. Lieberman, musician and *balabosta.*

RAT JACKET

WHENEVER MORE THAN ONE PERSON IS BEING PROSECUTED IN CONNECTION WITH THE SAME INCIDENT, THE RULE TO REMEMBER IS: NOBODY TALKS, EVERYBODY WALKS. UNFORTUNATELY FOR NICKI AND TENISHA, THEY RUN INTO AN OFFICER WHO'S GOOD AT FOOLING PEOPLE INTO THINKING THEIR FRIENDS HAVE SNITCHED ON THEM.

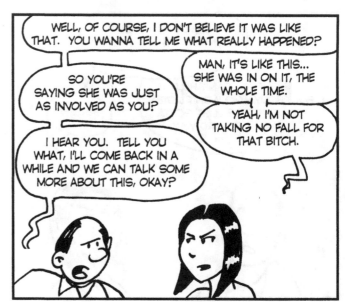

CHAPTER 5

PROBATION, PAROLE, AND SUPERVISED RELEASE

MY LAWYER MADE ME DO IT

WHEN YOU'RE UNDER COURT SUPERVISION (ON PROBATION, PAROLE OR SUPERVISED RELEASE), RESISTING INTERROGATION POSES SPECIAL PROBLEMS. JESSICA NEEDS TO FIGURE OUT THE BEST WAY TO SAY NO, WHEN POLICE, PROBATION OFFICERS AND PARENTS ARE ALL DEMANDING THAT SHE ANSWER QUESTIONS.

MS. IRVING? JOE LEE HERE. I GOT ONE OF YOUR CASES DOWN HERE, JESSICA NGUYEN. YEAH, GRAFFITI AGAIN. YOU WANNA SEE HER NOW? OKAY, YOU CAN HAVE HER WHILE I DO THE PAPERWORK.

YOUR PROBATION OFFICER IS ON HER WAY. NOW I GOTTA NOTIFY YOUR PARENTS.

HELLO, MAY I SPEAK TO MRS. MARY NGUYEN? MA'AM, WE HAVE YOUR DAUGHTER JESSICA IN CUSTODY. NO, I DON'T KNOW YET WHETHER SHE'S GOING TO BE RELEASED. IF YOU LIKE, I CAN GIVE YOU A CALL AFTER SHE'S BEEN PROCESSED. YOU WANNA COME IN? OKAY, YOU'RE WELCOME TO WAIT HERE. I'LL LET HER KNOW.

YOUR MOTHER'S ON HER WAY DOWN HERE, TOO.

LATER...

OFFICER LEE? WHAT SHE DO? SHE MAKE GRAFFITI AGAIN? I CANNOT BELIEVE SHE DO THAT AGAIN.

I'M AFRAID YOUR DAUGHTER HAS COMMITTED VANDALISM. AGAIN.

HER FATHER AND I TRY TO MAKE HER BEHAVE. WE HAVE GOOD HOME, GOOD FAMILY. I...I DON'T KNOW WHAT TO DO WITH HER.

WELL, THE BEST THING YOU CAN DO AT THIS POINT IS TO ENCOURAGE YOUR DAUGHTER TO TELL THE TRUTH. SHE'S BEEN HANGING OUT WITH SOME PRETTY BAD KIDS WHO'VE BEEN GETTING HER INTO TROUBLE. SHE NEEDS TO TALK TO US ABOUT WHAT REALLY HAPPENED.

JESSICA ANNE NGUYEN, I CANNOT BELIEVE YOU DO THIS AGAIN! HOW CAN YOU DO THIS TO ME?

YOU PROMISE YOU GOING TO BEHAVE, THEN YOU GO AND MAKE MORE GRAFFITI. I DON'T UNDERSTAND WHAT THE MATTER WITH YOU. YOU HAVE NICE HOME, NICE CLOTHES, NICE FOOD! WHY YOU GO MAKE GRAFFITI? YOU TELL ME!

MOM, PLEASE! IT'S ALL A MISTAKE, REALLY...

WELL, THAT WAS WORTHY OF AN OPRAH SHOW.

WHOEVER YOU ARE, UNLESS YOU HAVE SOMETHING CONSTRUCTIVE TO SAY, I'M NOT INTERESTED IN DEALING WITH YOU.

I APOLOGIZE. I SHOULD COMMEND YOU FOR COURAGE UNDER FIRE.

PARTICULARLY WHEN YOU'RE BEING ORDERED TO CONFESS BY THE POLICE, YOUR PROBATION OFFICER, AND YOUR MOM.

WELL, I WASN'T GOING TO SNITCH ON MY FRIENDS!

YOU DID BETTER THAN THAT. BY NOT ANSWERING QUESTIONS, YOU DIDN'T SNITCH ON YOURSELF, EITHER. I THINK, HOWEVER, THAT YOU COULD HAVE HANDLED THIS SITUATION WITH GREATER DIPLOMACY.

WHAT DO YOU MEAN? MY MOM WAS SO UPSET, IT WOULDN'T HAVE MATTERED WHAT I SAID.

PERHAPS NOT. ON THE OTHER HAND, YOU MIGHT HAVE GIVEN HER SOMETHING TO THINK ABOUT LATER, WHEN SHE COOLED DOWN. YOU COULD HAVE TOLD HER THAT YOU HAD BEEN TAUGHT TO SAY, I'M GOING TO REMAIN SILENT, I WOULD LIKE TO SEE A LAWYER. AND THAT IF SHE WOULD CALL A CRIMINAL DEFENSE LAWYER, SHE WOULD BE TOLD THAT YOU HAD DONE THE RIGHT THING.

BUT WHAT IF I DON'T HAVE A LAWYER?

REMEMBER, WHEN YOU INVOKE YOUR RIGHT TO SEE A LAWYER, YOU DON'T HAVE TO HAVE ONE ALREADY LINED UP. YOU CAN BE REFERRING TO A LAWYER THAT YOU'RE GOING TO HIRE, OR A LAWYER THAT THE COURT WILL APPOINT FOR YOU.

BUT ISN'T ASKING FOR A LAWYER GOING TO PISS OFF MY PROBATION OFFICER? SHE WAS HARSHING ON ME, TOO.

AND SHE SAID THAT IF SHE RECOMMENDED TO THE JUDGE TO LOCK ME UP, THE JUDGE WOULD JUST DO IT.

WELL, IT'S TRUE THAT JUDGES USUALLY FOLLOW THE PROBATION OFFICER'S RECOMMENDATION.

BUT THERE ARE WAYS KEEP THE PROBATION OFFICER FROM GETTING MAD AT YOU, WITHOUT SACRIFICING YOUR RIGHT TO REMAIN SILENT—AND THAT'S CRITICAL, BECAUSE WHATEVER YOU SAY TO THE PROBATION OFFICER WILL BE USED AGAINST YOU IN COURT.

THE EASIEST WAY TO HANDLE THE PROBATION OFFICER IS TO SAY THAT YOU'RE READY TO EXPLAIN EVERYTHING, BUT THAT YOU NEED TO GET YOUR LAWYER'S PERMISSION FIRST. ESSENTIALLY, YOU BLAME THE MEAN OLD LAWYER FOR THE FACT THAT YOU CAN'T JUST IMMEDIATELY SPILL YOUR GUTS TO THE PROBATION OFFICER.

AND EVEN IF I DON'T HAVE A LAWYER FOR MY NEW CASE, I COULD BE REFERRING TO MY LAST LAWYER, THE ONE FROM THE CASE I GOT PUT ON PROBATION FOR, RIGHT?

EXACTLY.

VERY TRUE, BUT YOU CAN HANDLE IT. YOU'VE GOT THAT STAR-QUALITY. HERE WE GO...

THIS STILL SOUNDS EASIER SAID THAN DONE. IT'S HARD TO MANIPULATE A CONVERSATION WHEN PEOPLE ARE YELLING AT YOU.

WHY YOU GO MAKE GRAFFITI? YOU TELL ME!

MOM, YOU HAVE A RIGHT TO BE UPSET. BUT I CAN'T TALK ABOUT WHAT HAPPENED RIGHT NOW. I'VE BEEN STUDYING CIVIL RIGHTS, AND WHAT I LEARNED IS THAT IN THIS SITUATION, I NEED TO REMAIN SILENT AND ASK FOR A LAWYER.

I KNOW YOU'RE MAD AT ME, BUT I ALSO KNOW THAT THIS IS WHAT I SHOULD DO RIGHT NOW.

YOU THINK YOU SO SMART, THEN WHAT YOU DOING HERE IN A POLICE STATION? MAYBE I OUGHT TO LEAVE YOU HERE, SO YOU CAN LEARN SOME RESPECT.

I DO RESPECT YOU, MOM, AND I LOVE YOU. I UNDERSTAND THAT YOU DON'T TRUST WHAT I'M TELLING YOU AND THAT YOU MAY DECIDE TO LEAVE ME HERE. ALL I ASK IS THAT YOU SPEAK TO A CRIMINAL DEFENSE LAWYER FIRST, BEFORE YOU MAKE A FINAL DECISION. IF THE LAWYER SAYS THAT I'M DOING THE RIGHT THING BY REMAINING SILENT AND ASKING FOR AN ATTORNEY, THEN COME BACK AND GET ME.

JESSICA, WHAT IS GOING ON WITH YOU? I NEED AN EXPLANATION OF JUST WHAT YOU THOUGHT YOU WERE DOING. YOU KNOW, I KEPT YOU FROM GETTING LOCKED UP THE LAST TIME YOU ENGAGED IN VANDALISM, BUT I'M HAVING SECOND THOUGHTS...

MS. IRVING, I'M SO GLAD YOU'RE HERE. I REMEMBER HOW MUCH YOU HELPED ME BEFORE, AND I REALLY WANT TO TELL YOU WHAT JUST HAPPENED...

BUT I'M KIND OF NERVOUS ABOUT MY ATTORNEY. SHE'S REALLY STRICT AND SHE TOLD ME THAT I COULDN'T MAKE ANY STATEMENTS WITHOUT HER BEING THERE. I'M AFRAID OF GETTING HER ANGRY WITH ME. COULD YOU CALL HER AND LET HER KNOW THAT I'M HERE? I JUST NEED TO GET HER PERMISSION, AND THEN I CAN EXPLAIN EVERYTHING...

WELL, I KNOW SOME ATTORNEYS ARE LIKE THAT. LET'S SEE IF WE CAN ARRANGE A TIME THAT I CAN TALK TO YOU WITH HER HERE AS WELL.

I KNEW YOU'D UNDERSTAND...

THAT WAS AN OSCAR-WINNING PERFORMANCE. MOST IMPRESSIVE.

I WAS GOOD, WASN'T I? OF COURSE, IF I DID HAVE AN ATTORNEY PRESENT, SHE WOULDN'T LET ME "EXPLAIN EVERYTHING"— JUST WHAT IT WAS SAFE TO SAY.

OF COURSE. THERE'S NO NEED TO OVER-SHARE.

DO YOU THINK MY MOM WOULD'VE DONE THAT TOUGH-LOVE THING AND LEFT ME THERE?

THAT'S HARD TO SAY. YOU KNOW YOUR MOM BETTER THAN I DO. BUT ONCE SHE DOES TALK TO A CRIMINAL DEFENSE LAWYER, SHE'LL BE TOLD FOR SURE THAT YOU WERE DOING THE RIGHT THING. AND BY THEN SHE'LL HAVE HAD TIME TO COOL DOWN. SO MAYBE YOU WOULD END UP BEING LEFT IN CUSTODY FOR A LITTLE WHILE—BUT THAT'S BETTER THAN DOING A LOT OF TIME LATER ON, BECAUSE YOU LOST THE CASE BY MAKING A STATEMENT TO THE PROBATION OFFICER.

COURT SUPERVISION

"Formal probation"[1] is a period of time, usually ranging from six months to five years, in which a convicted person remains under the court's control. The conditions of probation generally include:

- reporting regularly to a supervising officer

- obeying all laws

- restrictions on where you can go

- restrictions on whom you can associate with

- drug testing

- attendance at classes, counseling, or meetings

- submission to searches *without* probable cause

- payment of fines and/or restitution

People who work in the legal system frequently use jargon when discussing conditions of supervision. This may involve abbreviations for stay-away orders or for types of searches to which you must submit. Make sure you get a clear explanation of the terms of supervision before you agree to it. This is one of those areas in which ignorance of the law is definitely no excuse.

If you violate one of these conditions, the judge may impose additional restrictions and/or lengthen your period of probation—she might even send you to jail or prison. Generally, the judge relies heavily on the recommendation of your probation officer, who will submit a report upon request of the judge or prosecutor. Note that probation violation hearings are very different from real trials. At such a hearing, you're not entitled to a jury—the judge alone decides whether you've violated your probation. What's more, the judge is not required to find you guilty beyond a reasonable doubt, but can base the decision on a much lower standard of proof, such as "preponderance of the evidence" or "reasonable certainty."

"Parole" is a period of supervision following release from a state prison. "Supervised release" is a period of supervision following release from federal prison. Both involve conditions and penalties of the type discussed above. If you're charged with violating your conditions, you only get a hearing, not a jury trial. At the violation hearing, the decision maker may be a parole board, rather than a judge, but the recommendation of the supervising officer will still carry a great deal of weight.

So, if you're under some form of supervision and you get arrested, you've got two problems. First, you've got a whole new case; second, you're likely to face a hearing on whether you've violated the conditions of supervision from your previous case, by breaking the law, etc.

Now, sometimes you only suffer one penalty. For example, if you're on probation and you get arrested, the prosecutor may not bother to file new charges against you, but may simply petition that your probation be revoked. That's advantageous for the prosecutor, because you're only entitled to a quick hearing rather than a full trial.

---

1. Informal probation, sometimes called "court probation," may include most of these conditions, but does not involve reporting to a probation officer.

On the other hand, you could be convicted and sentenced on the new case; and then be found in violation of your probation or parole, and sentenced for that as well. The authorities don't always bother to punish you twice, but they can.

Naturally, if you fight the new case and win, you're not likely to be found in violation of your conditions of supervision. It is possible, however, to violate a condition—such as staying away from a certain location—without violating the law. So a vindictive prosecutor or judge could still make trouble for you, even if you were acquitted of the new charges.

SEARCHES WHILE UNDER SUPERVISION

Most forms of supervision include a condition giving law enforcement officers the right to search without probable cause or even reasonable suspicion. That is, while under court supervision, you generally lose the protection of the Fourth Amendment. Typically, searches while under supervision include: searches of your person, your home, your vehicle and your workplace. This has particular significance for those who live with you. If you're on probation, parole, or supervised release, an officer can come into your home—without reason or warning—and search not just your bedroom, but also the common areas: kitchen, bathroom, family room, etc. Although it can be awkward to discuss these things with roommates and family, it's safer for everyone (including you) if all the people you live with understand the added risk to their privacy.

INTERVIEWS WITH SUPERVISING OFFICERS

If you're arrested while on probation, parole or court supervision, you'll normally be interviewed by your supervising officer—and anything you say will be used against you in a court of law. So it's critical that you use your rights to remain silent and see an attorney. Of course, you need to maintain a good relationship with the officer, because you don't want him to recommend to the judge that you go to jail. If at all possible, contact a lawyer as soon as you're arrested and ask for help in dealing with the supervising officer. Ideally, get your lawyer to come to the interview. Failing that, get the lawyer to give you specific advice on what to say.[2] If you end up seeing the supervising officer *before* you've had a chance to talk to your lawyer, explain that that you need to get your lawyer's permission, before answering questions, because you don't want to get your lawyer mad at you. And be very respectful. (See how Jessica does it in *My Lawyer Made Me Do It,* page 68.)

---

2. If you're represented by a public defender, she probably won't have time to see the supervising officer with you, but may be able to give you advice on what to talk about.

CHAPTER

6

UNDERCOVER OFFICERS, INFORMANTS, AND ENTRAPMENT

LET ME ASK YOU THIS: IF UNDERCOVER POLICE OFFICERS HAD TO ADMIT THEY WERE COPS ANYTIME SOMEONE ASKED THEM, HOW COULD THEY GET THEIR JOBS DONE? THINK ABOUT IT.

BUT, DON'T THE COPS GOT TO FOLLOW THE RULES? I MEAN, THAT AIN'T FAIR.

TRY AGAIN. IF THE RULE WERE THAT AN UNDERCOVER OFFICER HAS TO ANSWER TRUTHFULLY WHENEVER ANYONE ASKS IF HE'S A COP, WOULD HE BE ABLE TO REMAIN UNDERCOVER? WOULD HE EVER BE ABLE TO BUST ANYONE?

I GUESS NOT. BUT IT STILL AIN'T FAIR.

MAYBE NOT, BUT THAT'S THE LAW: OFFICERS WORKING UNDERCOVER ARE ALLOWED TO LIE ABOUT THEIR IDENTITY.

OKAY, OKAY. BUT HE SMOKED THAT WEED WITH ME. YOU SAW HIM. I ASKED HIM TO SMOKE SOME WITH ME, YOU KNOW, TO PROVE HE WASN'T NO NARC. AND HE DID SMOKE SOME.

OKAY, NOW THINK LOGICALLY ABOUT THIS. SINCE IT'S LEGAL FOR UNDERCOVER POLICE TO LIE ABOUT BEING COPS, WOULDN'T IT MAKE SENSE FOR UNDERCOVER NARCOTICS OFFICERS TO BE ABLE TO DO DRUGS? DON'T YOU THINK IT WOULD BE HARD FOR NARCS TO PLAY THEIR ROLES, ESPECIALLY OVER A LONG-TERM INVESTIGATION, IF THEY COULDN'T DO DRUGS?

OH, MAN. WHAT YOU'RE SAYING IS, THERE'S NO WAY, JUST NO WAY, TO TELL WHO'S A NARC AND WHO AIN'T.

AND YOU'RE SURE ABOUT THIS? YOU'RE SURE THIS IS ALL LEGAL, WHAT HE DONE TO ME?

I AM AN ORACLE. OF COURSE, IF YOU DON'T WANT TO TAKE MY WORD FOR IT, BY ALL MEANS, TAKE THIS CASE TO TRIAL.

BUT I'M TELLING YOU, YOU WON'T WIN THIS ONE IN COURT IF YOU'RE ARGUING ENTRAPMENT. HOW ABOUT I GIVE YOU A SECOND CHANCE? A CHANCE TO PROVE YOU'VE LEARNED SOMETHING?

YEAH, WHATEVER.

UNDERCOVER OFFICERS

There is no reliable way to identify undercover agents or informants. The good ones act entirely in keeping with their roles. An experienced undercover officer is not going to seem unduly nervous, wear inappropriate clothing, or fumble with the drugs he's handling.

Undercover officers are legally allowed to lie when you inquire whether they're law enforcement personnel. It does no good to ask, "Are you a cop?" Undercover cops can just reply, "Of course not." After all, if they couldn't lie, it would be a waste of effort for law enforcement agencies to train and disguise all those officers for undercover roles—they'd be exposed early on, every time they tried to pass.

It's perfectly legal for undercover officers and informants to engage in criminal activity to protect their cover. Narcs are allowed to buy, sell and do drugs of every kind. Forget any urban myths you may have heard to the contrary: narcs are entitled to smoke/snort/swallow/inject controlled substances. Similarly, vice officers investigating prostitution are allowed to get naked and receive "massage." (It's good to know that your tax dollars are being well-spent.)[2]

Although many undercover officers and informants come equipped with transmitting or recording devices, this type of electronic equipment is miniaturized. A police agent who's "wearing a wire" is unlikely to be uncovered by mere patting. The equipment can easily be hidden in hard articles of clothing, such as belt buckles, boots, etc. Of course, undercover officers and informants don't have to be wired for sound, they can just report from memory (accurately or not) about whatever they've seen and heard.

INFORMANTS

Law enforcement agencies often use informants. Some informants work for money, but most are people who've been caught engaging in criminal activity. The vast majority of snitch deals are made by the police, who refrain from charging a suspect they've caught, in return for information or undercover work (typically, buying or selling drugs). A much smaller number of snitch deals are made by the police and the prosecutor together, when the suspect has criminal charges pending or is serving time. In these situations, the prosecutor lowers the charges or seeks to reduce the sentence, in return for information or undercover work.

---

1. Undercover officers find it a particularly useful tactic to mention that they're worried about the police, occasionally asking the suspect whether *he's* a cop—the ol' switcheroo

2. Most people are surprised to learn that law enforcement agents can, as part of their job, lie and engage in criminal activity. It seems unfair that the police don't have to live up to the same standards they're enforcing. However, a great deal of police investigation operates on the basis that the end justifies the means—a flawed rationale, particularly in the context of maintaining a just legal system. Crooked tools build a crooked structure.

It's not worth it to law enforcement agencies to use snitches in investigating misdemeanors—they want information leading to felony convictions. In choosing a snitch, law enforcement agents look for someone who has significant criminal experience (a long rap sheet), because such a person is likely to have good connections and also seem relaxed and natural while participating in undercover work. Occasionally, officers will use a less-experienced snitch, if that person has a really good connection to the particular target of their investigation. A very productive snitch will be protected by law enforcement, to maintain him as a source of future information. An inept snitch may not be so lucky.

Informants can be very deceptive since they're usually quite at home with the activities and communities they're working on. In fact, an informant can be an old friend or acquaintance who only just recently happened to fall under police control. Even though you know that someone's been quietly selling drugs for many years, there's no guarantee that he hasn't just as quietly become an informant in the past month. Some informants are prisoners (or cops pretending to be prisoners), put into the same cell as an incarcerated suspect. Just as with undercover officers, informants do not admit that they're really law enforcement agents in disguise.

INFILTRATORS

Infiltrators are undercover officers or informants who become members of political organizations. Some infiltrators just report on the other members of the organization (who they are, what they're doing). Other infiltrators actively undermine the political organization, by causing dissension among the members or by promoting risky, harmful activities. An infiltrator who pushes other activists to engage in behavior that's contrary to the organization's goals or ethical standards is an "agent provocateur." Just a few of the organizations that have suffered from government infiltration are: the AFL-CIO, the Black Panthers, the Committee in Solidarity with the People of El Salvador (CISPES), and Earth First! A huge and particularly well-documented infiltration and disruption program was COINTELPRO, a long-term FBI operation.

Some activists, at the beginning of meetings, mistakenly announce: "Will all law enforcement agents please identify themselves?" Needless to say, no one comes forward. Aside from being futile, this ritual gives participants a false sense of security, as they may imagine that their meeting is therefore entirely free from surveillance.

ENTRAPMENT

An undercover officer can legally initiate crime. That is, the narc can be the person pushing the drugs, or actively seeking a source for buying them. ("Hey man, you know where I can get some good weed? Can you hook me up?")

Most people imagine that when an undercover law enforcement officer instigates a crime, that's entrapment. Unfortunately, "entrapment" is one of those words that has a much narrower definition in a court of law than in common speech. To argue at trial that a criminal defendant was entrapped into committing a crime, the defense attorney has to get permission from the judge in advance. She has to show that the defendant (1) had no inclination or tendency to commit the crime, and (2) that the law enforcement agent(s) exerted considerable psychological pressure to get the defendant to break the law. Unfortunately, when the defendant has prior convictions or even arrests, the prosecutor often successfully argues that the defendant has demonstrated criminal tendencies. Moreover, it's hard to show that the defendant was urged so intensely that he eventually caved in and agreed to commit the crime. For example, in the preceding story, *Narc in the Park*, Jamal wouldn't be successful in arguing that the undercover officer overwhelmed him into buying the marijuana. By contrast, consider the following two cases which show how much evidence is required to prove entrapment.

Entrapment Example 1: Postal inspectors, pretending to be a variety of different sellers of pornography, spent over two years persuading a man to send away for obscene photos. The court ruled that this was entrapment.

Entrapment Example 2: An informant in a drug treatment program, after much pleading and insistence that he was truly suffering because the treatment wasn't working for him, eventually convinced a fellow patient to get drugs for him. The court ruled that this was entrapment.[3]

---

3. In every city, undercover law enforcement agents are spending their time encouraging and assisting people to engage in criminal activity, to see who's going to fall from grace. Instead of helping to maintain a healthy society, they're picking at scabs on the body politic.

DEALING WITH ARREST WARRANTS AND SEARCH WARRANTS

WHAT'S WORSE THAN HAVING A COUPLE OF POLICE OFFICERS ON YOUR PORCH, ABOUT TO ARREST YOU? HAVING THE OFFICERS IN YOUR BEDROOM, DISCOVERING EVIDENCE THAT WILL LEAD TO ADDITIONAL CHARGES. THAT'S WHAT HAPPENS WHEN JAMES MAKES THE WRONG MOVE IN

DO NOT PASS GO, DO NOT COLLECT $200

There's some overlap between arrest warrants and search warrants. An arrest warrant allows law enforcement officers to take you into custody—and following arrest, you and your immediate surroundings can be searched. By contrast, a search warrant allows law enforcement officers to search a particular place (home, business, vehicle, or person)—and sometimes the search reveals items that give the officers grounds for arresting you. Finally, judges can issue combined search and arrest warrants. (See a sample arrest warrant on page 88 and sample search warrants beginning on page 97.)

ARREST WARRANTS

Arrest warrants generally arise when either:

(1) The police ask a judge to issue an arrest warrant on the grounds that there's probable cause that the suspect committed a crime, or

(2) A defendant or witness fails to show up for court, so the judge issues an arrest warrant for that person. (These are called "bench warrants" since the judge issues them while sitting in court.)

Unlike search warrants, which are normally valid for only a week or two, arrest warrants can remain valid for years. Databases of arrest warrants exist in county, state and federal computer systems. When a suspect is detained or arrested, the officers generally run a computer search to see whether there are any warrants for that person. Searches of the arrest warrant records for a particular state can often be accomplished within a matter of minutes—for instance, while you're waiting for the police to write you a ticket after they pulled you over for a traffic violation. A search that checks all the states and/or the federal system takes somewhat longer. Police and prosecutors don't always bother to check beyond their own state, particularly in misdemeanor cases.

If there's an arrest warrant out for you because you're the target of a criminal investigation, it may be difficult to find out about it in advance. The officers who hope to arrest you will want to keep the warrant a secret, lest you go into hiding. A bench warrant, however, is a public record and you can verify whether one has been issued.

If you think there might be a bench warrant out for you, but you're not sure, it's safest to have a criminal defense lawyer or a bail bondsman check for you. Depending on the jurisdiction and charge, you may risk being arrested

if you go and ask about warrants and it turns out that there is one. If you're not able to get professional help, you can try asking the "clerk of the court" who handles criminal records (not civil records). It may be possible to do this over the phone, but usually you have to go to the courthouse and deal with the clerk in person to get help. Make sure you're looking in the right court system. If you think there's a federal case against you, talk to the clerk of the U.S. District Court. If you think there's a state case, talk to the clerk of the county court—preferably the county the charges were filed in.

If there *is* a warrant out for your arrest, you may want to deal with the underlying case, so that you don't have it hanging over your head. Usually, this involves going to court. It's generally worthwhile to have a lawyer help set up the hearing and speak on your behalf. If you're low-income, contact the public defender's office of the county in which the warrant was issued. Meet with the duty attorney[1] and explain that you want to clear your warrant. It will speed things up if you know the case number associated with your warrant.

If police officers come to the door with an arrest warrant for you, step outside and lock the door. Don't go back inside after you're in custody, or the police will be able to search the wingspan area[2] of every room you enter. In addition, the officers could do a "protective sweep," checking the whole house to make sure you don't have an accomplice waiting to attack them. So don't go back indoors to get your wallet or use the bathroom. Even if you're not wearing much clothing, it's safer to go to the police station as you are, than to let the officers into your home.

The reason for this is that you simply never know whether the police might find something in your house that could be used against you in court. Just because there's no contraband (such as illegal drugs or weapons) in your home doesn't mean it's safe to let the police inside. Some seemingly unimportant item—a jacket, a key, a telephone list—might be used to link you with a crime.[3] Besides, a family member, roommate, or friend could have left contraband in your home that you didn't know about—and you might not be able to convince a judge or jury that this happened without your knowledge or permission. What's more, there have been cases in which corrupt officers planted drugs or other incriminating items in a suspect's home. So it's best not to let law enforcement agents inside if you can avoid it—and

---

1. In most public defender's offices, the attorneys take turns being the one who answers questions from people who call or drop in—that lawyer is usually called the "duty attorney."

2. Your wingspan is the space within your immediate control (the area within lunging distance).

3. Harmless-looking objects can turn out to be damaging in court, just as harmless-sounding statements can turn out to be incriminating (like Justin's statements in *Use a Pie, Go to Jail*, page 46).

one way to avoid it is to step outside immediately and go with the police if they show up with an arrest warrant.

Of course, it's important to make sure that the police *do* have an arrest warrant for you, before leaving the safety of your home. If you answer the door and the police say, "Come on outside, so we can talk to you," then it's likely that they don't have a warrant and are just trying to lure you out—where they can easily detain, question and pat search you, in the hope of finding grounds for arrest. You should say no, close the door, and call a criminal defense attorney.

Remember that when the officers do have an arrest warrant for you, hiding in your house won't help, because police are allowed to force their way in to get you if they believe you're in there. In that case, you might as well go outside and let them take you into custody, without letting them search your house or break your front door. (And at this point you should say: *I'm going to remain silent. I would like to see a lawyer.*)

Smart law enforcement officers will verify that the suspect is in a particular location, and cover all the exits, before they serve the arrest warrant. They may keep the house or apartment under surveillance until the suspect arrives, wait for him to go inside, and then serve the arrest warrant. This increases the chances that the police will get to go inside and look around—which the officers might not get to do, if they just arrested the suspect on his way to the door.

Of course, sometimes the police arrest the wrong person, especially when people share the same name or look alike. It's very hard to convince the police, at the time they're arresting you, that you're not the person specified in the warrant. So if the police believe you're the person for whom the warrant was issued, resign yourself to going to the station and don't argue. Anything you say will be used against you in court, and the more you talk to the police, the more likely you'll say something that can hurt you—even if you're innocent. Just stick with the Magic Words, *I'm going to remain silent. I would like to see a lawyer.* If it's a matter of mistaken identity, you and your lawyer can get the matter straightened out in court. Slowly but surely wins the case.

COUNTY OF METROPOLIS, STATE OF WEST DAKOTA

ARREST WARRANT   Case No. 03-1745

The People of the State of West Dakota, to any peace officer; proof by affidavit having been made before me on this date by Officer J. Friendly, Metropolis Police Department, that there is probable cause to believe that the offense of Penal Code section 312(d) (Burglary) was committed on or about March 15, 2003, by:

CHRISTOPHER SMITH
   a.k.a. Chris Smith
   a.k.a. Kris Smith
   a.k.a. A.J. Raffles

Race:	BLK	DOB: 5/1/70
Sex:	M	DL#:
Ht:	6'1"	Ph:
Wt:	175	
Hair:	BLK	Add: 403 Bank St.
Eyes:	BRN	Metropolis, WD 20535

YOU ARE THEREFORE ORDERED TO ARREST the defendant and bring him or her forthwith to the nearest magistrate.

_$30,000—_
Bail Amount

_4/1/03   2:30 pm._   _Roy Bean_
Date/Time   Signature of Magistrate

RETURN

This warrant was received and executed with the arrest of the above-named defendant at

403 BANK ST., METROPOLIS, WD

_4/1/03_   _J. FRIENDLY_   _J. Friendly_
Date Received   Name of Arresting Officer   Signature of Arresting Officer

_4/2/03_
Date of Arrest

WHEN THE POLICE SHOW UP WITH A WARRANT, EVERYONE KNOWS YOU'RE SUPPOSED TO READ IT. BUT WHAT DO YOU LOOK FOR? HOW DO YOU TELL IF THE WARRANT'S VALID? MARIA FACES THIS PROBLEM WHEN THE POLICE COME TO

SEARCH AND DESTROY

THINK OF THIS AS A TIME OUT. AND BEFORE YOU GO BACK IN THE GAME, YOU NEED SOME COACHING. LET'S START BY TALKING ABOUT WHERE THINGS STARTED TO GO WRONG.

WHEN THE POLICE SHOWED UP AT MY DOOR WITH A SEARCH WARRANT?

PARTLY RIGHT. WHAT DID YOU DO AT THAT POINT?

I LET THEM IN. WHAT ELSE COULD I DO?

DID YOU LOOK AT THE WARRANT?

NO. THEY DIDN'T SHOW IT TO ME. THEY JUST CAME RIGHT IN.

BUT YOU DIDN'T EVEN ASK TO SEE THE WARRANT, DID YOU?

I GUESS NOT. WOULD THEY HAVE SHOWN IT TO ME?

MAYBE. IT COULDN'T HURT TO ASK.

BUT I DON'T EVEN KNOW WHAT TO LOOK FOR ON A WARRANT, I MEAN, YOU KNOW, TO SEE IF IT'S OKAY.

WELL, FOR STARTERS, IT SHOULD SAY "SEARCH WARRANT" ON IT. IT HAS TO BE SIGNED BY A JUDGE OR MAGISTRATE. IT HAS TO BE DATED, AND THE DATE HAS TO BE REASONABLY RECENT— MORE THAN A COUPLE OF WEEKS BACK IS PROBABLY TOO OLD. AND, OF COURSE, THE WARRANT HAS TO HAVE THE RIGHT ADDRESS ON IT.

WHAT DO YOU MEAN, THE RIGHT ADDRESS? HOW COULD THEY COME IN AND SEARCH, IF THEY DON'T HAVE THE RIGHT ADDRESS?

ACCIDENTS HAPPEN. SOMETIMES ON PURPOSE.

OH, MAN! BUT THEY DON'T ALWAYS EVEN NEED A WARRANT, DO THEY? I THOUGHT THEY COULD JUST GO ON IN SOMETIMES?

YOU'RE RIGHT—THE POLICE CAN ENTER AND SEARCH WITHOUT A WARRANT IF, FOR EXAMPLE, THEY'RE IN HOT PURSUIT OF A SERIOUS CRIMINAL, OR THEY'RE RESPONDING TO A CRY FOR HELP.

ON THE OTHER HAND, LOTS OF TIMES THEY DON'T NEED A WARRANT BECAUSE SOMEONE GIVES CONSENT FOR THEM TO COME IN.

RIGHT, LIKE THEY'RE GOING TO ASK.

NO, REALLY, SOMETIMES THEY DO ASK FOR YOUR CONSENT, AS IN: "MIND IF WE COME IN AND HAVE A LOOK AROUND?"

OTHER TIMES, IT SOUNDS MORE LIKE A STATEMENT OR AN ORDER: "WE'RE JUST GONNA CHECK THIS PLACE OUT, IT'LL ONLY TAKE MINUTE." BUT ONCE YOU SAY OKAY, THEN YOU DON'T GET TO ARGUE IN COURT THAT THE POLICE DIDN'T HAVE A PROPER WARRANT OR A VALID REASON TO SEARCH WITHOUT ONE. SOMETIMES LAWYERS CAN GET EVIDENCE SUPPRESSED, IF A SEARCH TURNS OUT TO HAVE BEEN ILLEGAL. BUT IF YOU GIVE CONSENT, THEN ANY SEARCH IS LEGAL.

DO I HAVE TO ACTUALLY SAY, "OKAY, YOU CAN COME IN," FOR THEM TO HAVE MY CONSENT? I MEAN, WHAT IF I JUST DIDN'T SAY ANYTHING?

THAT'S AN INTERESTING QUESTION. AND THE ANSWER IS, YOU SHOULD PUT YOUR REFUSAL TO CONSENT IN WORDS—BECAUSE SILENCE CAN OFTEN BE INTERPRETED AS AGREEMENT.

BESIDES, THE POLICE MIGHT CLAIM THAT YOU NODDED AS THOUGH TO GIVE PERMISSION. OR THAT YOU STEPPED AWAY FROM THE DOOR, SORT OF WELCOMING THE POLICE IN.

IS THERE A RIGHT OR A WRONG WAY TO SAY IT? LIKE, SHOULD I BE ALL FORMAL AND SAY, "YOU DO NOT HAVE MY CONSENT TO COME IN. YOU DO NOT HAVE MY CONSENT TO SEARCH?"

ACTUALLY, THAT'S AN EXCELLENT WAY TO PUT IT.

OKAY, SO I TELL THE POLICE FORMALLY, "YOU DON'T HAVE MY CONSENT TO SEARCH." BUT WHAT IF THEY DON'T NEED MY CONSENT. WHAT IF THEY HAVE A REAL WARRANT, OR ONE OF THOSE EXCEPTIONS WHERE THEY DON'T NEED A WARRANT?

THE GOOD NEWS IS, REFUSING CONSENT CANNOT HURT. IT CAN'T BE USED AGAINST YOU IN COURT.

AND IF THE POLICE DO GO AHEAD AND SEARCH WITHOUT A VALID REASON, THEN YOU'LL HAVE GIVEN YOUR LAWYER A VALUABLE TOOL FOR SUPPRESSING THE EVIDENCE COLLECTED DURING THE SEARCH. GO AHEAD AND SAY REPEATEDLY THAT YOU DON'T CONSENT. TRY TO SAY IT IN FRONT OF WITNESSES.

OKAY, OKAY, SO I TELL THE POLICE, "YOU DON'T HAVE MY CONSENT TO SEARCH." WHAT HAPPENS IF THEY JUST PUSH RIGHT PAST ME? THAT'S WHAT THEY DID BEFORE. I'M NOT SUPPOSED TO TRY TO STOP THEM, AM I?

ABSOLUTELY NOT! NEVER PUSH OR EVEN TOUCH A POLICE OFFICER. YOU'D BE CHARGED WITH RESISTING, IF NOT BATTERY, AND YOU'D PROBABLY GET HURT.

WHAT YOU CAN DO IS TO KEEP THE DOOR CLOSED AND TALK THROUGH IT, OR KEEP THE CHAIN ON, IF THERE IS ONE, WHILE YOU TALK. OR, YOU COULD SLIP OUTSIDE AND CLOSE THE DOOR BEHIND YOU, AND THEN DEAL WITH THE POLICE. IT MAKES SENSE TO AVOID BEING IN A POSITION WHERE THE OFFICERS CAN JUST SHOVE YOU ASIDE AND COME IN.

I DON'T KNOW. IT'S A LOT TO KEEP TRACK OF. THERE'S SO MANY THINGS THAT COULD GO WRONG...

THAT'S TRUE. BUT I'M CONVINCED THAT YOU CAN HANDLE IT. IF YOU CONCENTRATE, YOU'LL DO JUST FINE. NOW GET IN THERE AND USE YOUR HEAD.

WE HAVE A SEARCH WARRANT FOR THIS APARTMENT. IS THERE ANYONE ELSE HOME?

COULD I SEE THE WARRANT, PLEASE?

DON'T WORRY, WE'VE GOT A WARRANT ALL RIGHT.

THEN YOU WON'T MIND SHOWING IT TO ME? IT'LL JUST TAKE A MINUTE.

THANK YOU VERY MUCH. I APPRECIATE YOUR LETTING ME SEE THIS....

SEARCH WARRANTS

Search warrants allow law enforcement agents to search a particular place (or vehicle or person) and seize items that might have evidentiary value. To obtain a search warrant, an officer must show a judge that there's probable cause that a crime has been or is being committed. The officer's "affidavit," or statement of probable cause, is usually submitted to the court in writing, but sometimes an officer gives her affidavit orally, usually when calling from a crime scene to request a warrant. (For an example of probable cause, see Arrest, page 5.)

The general rule is that the police are required to "knock and announce" when serving a search warrant, as in: [knock, knock] "Ma'am, this is the police. We have a search warrant for these premises." If you then refuse to let the officers in, they have the right to force the door open.

The police are allowed to skip the knock and announce part when they reasonably believe that officers would be endangered or evidence destroyed, should the occupants have any warning. Even when they do knock and announce, they may only wait a few seconds before bursting in.

If police knock on your door and state that they have a search warrant, step outside and close the door behind you, then ask them to give you the warrant so you can read it. (If you stand inside with the door open, the police may just push past you before you can react.) Make sure you actually get your hands on the warrant so you can read it properly. Don't let the officer just wave it in front of you.[4]

You're looking for three things, to be sure it's a valid warrant:

* the address
* the date
* the judge's signature

Address: checking that the warrant really does have your address on it is the most important thing. Police frequently search the wrong house or apartment, and claim it was just a mistake. Note that a warrant can't be for a whole apartment building or floor—it has to be for a specific apartment.

Date: the date should not generally be older than two weeks. There isn't a precise number of days that warrants are good for. They can be served as long as a reasonable officer would expect to find the items listed in the warrant. Some judges have held that a particular warrant was valid even after a month or two, but these were rare cases. For simplicity's sake, most police departments just make a rule for themselves about how many days the officers can wait before serving a search warrant—usually it's seven or ten days.

Signature: it's pretty unusual for a warrant to lack a judge's or magistrate's[5] signature, but it could happen.

Warrants come in a wide variety of formats. Take a look at the sample search warrants, page 97, and see how quickly you can spot the address, date, and signature. (While you're looking for these items, imagine that you're standing in front of your door, with police officers breathing down your neck.) The address is hardest, because it's often in the middle of a paragraph. The date and signature will be at the end.

If you do find a flaw in the warrant, show it to the police and tell them that you don't consent to their coming in. For example, you might say:

* This warrant is for a different address: it's for 1965 Montgomery St., and my house is 1966 Montgomery. I don't consent to your coming in.

* This house has apartments in it. Your warrant doesn't say whether it's for Unit A or Unit B, so it's no good. I don't consent to your coming in.

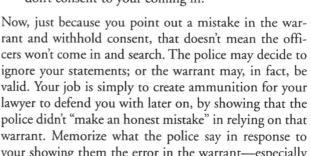

* This warrant is four months old. It's not valid anymore. I don't consent to your coming in.

* This warrant doesn't have a judge's signature, so it's not valid. I don't consent to your coming in.

* This is a laundry receipt, not a search warrant. I don't consent to your coming in.

Now, just because you point out a mistake in the warrant and withhold consent, that doesn't mean the officers won't come in and search. The police may decide to ignore your statements; or the warrant may, in fact, be valid. Your job is simply to create ammunition for your lawyer to defend you with later on, by showing that the police didn't "make an honest mistake" in relying on that warrant. Memorize what the police say in response to your showing them the error in the warrant—especially if it's something like, "I don't give a shit what your address is."

---

4. If the police kick the door in and point guns at you, screaming, "Police! Down on the floor, nobody move," you can skip attempting to read the warrant, and instead just keep your hands in view and hold very still.

5. A magistrate is a subspecies of judge.

There are other parts to a search warrant that may be relevant during the course of defending a criminal case, but they're not as useful while the police are right at your door. For example, search warrants must specify what is being looked for and which parts of your home, vehicle, etc. can be searched. However, as you can see in the samples, search warrants usually have a whole long list of things to look for and places to look in. This gives the police plenty of room to maneuver. Nonetheless, you should make notes (written notes if possible, otherwise mental notes) about where the officers search and what they move.

Normally, search warrants must be executed during daylight hours, unless the warrant includes specific permission for the officers to serve it at night.

While executing the search warrant, the officers are allowed to detain anyone who happens to be present. The police can pat down the people they're detaining,[6] but cannot search any of them more intrusively, unless the warrant specifies that particular person by name. (The second of the sample search warrants, page 100, includes a person to be searched, as well as a place.) However, it's not unusual for police who are searching pursuant to a warrant, to discover things that give them probable cause to arrest some or all of the people present—and once a suspect's been arrested, the officers can search her clothing, body, etc.

Some search warrants include permission for the officers to answer your telephone while they're on the premises searching. The police pretend to be you, or someone who's a part of your household, business, etc. They try to get the caller to say things that can be used against you (or against the caller) in court.

Most searches are very destructive. Your property is likely to be thrown about and damaged. So after the police have gone, take three or four dozen photographs of the place, before doing any clean-up. These may be useful in defending against criminal charges and/or in suing the police. Make sure you've got good enough lighting that the photos will come out well.

---

6. During a detention (as opposed to an arrest), the police are only allowed to pat down the suspect, in order to protect themselves from hidden weapons. This search is limited to feeling the surface of clothing, and does not include emptying the suspect's pockets or undressing the suspect. See Detention, page 4.

COUNTY OF METROPOLIS, STATE OF WEST DAKOTA

SEARCH WARRANT   NO. 31415

The People of the State of West Dakota, to any sheriff or police officer in the County of Metropolis; proof by affidavit having been made before me by Officer J. Friendly that there is probable cause to believe that the property or things described herein may be found at the locations set forth and that such property is seizable under 1066 P.C. in that it:

___   Was stolen or embezzled;

_X_   Was used as a means of committing a felony;

_X_   is possessed by a person with the intent to use it as a means of committing a public offense; or is possessed by another to whom he/she may have delivered it for the purpose of concealing it or preventing its discovery;

_X_   is evidence which tends to show that a felony has been committed or a particular person has committed a felony;

___   is evidence which tends to show sexual exploitation of a child, in violation of Penal Code section 456, has occurred or is occurring;

YOU ARE THEREFORE COMMANDED TO SEARCH:

The premises and building known and designated as and commonly called:

102 3rd St., Metropolis, West Dakota, more particularly described as a light blue two-story house, with white trim. 102 3rd St. is located at the south end of the first block of 3rd St.

including all rooms, attics, and other parts therein, garages, storage rooms, and outbuildings used in connection with the premises or located thereon and in any receptacle or safe therein;

for the following:

1. Books, receipts, ledgers, and other records tending to identify customers and other records that are consistent with prostitution of individual women employed at the business at 102 3rd St., Metropolis, West Dakota;

2. Employment applications, employer/employee contracts, time cards or other recordings tending to identify employees located at 102 3rd St., Metropolis, West Dakota;

3. Personal and business checks, monies and other evidence of debts owed pertaining to business transactions located at 102 3rd St., Metropolis, West Dakota, and/or financial records;

4. Contraceptive devices, used and unused, consisting in part of and including, but not limited to, condoms, diaphragms, anti-spermatozoa jellies and foams;

5. Sexual paraphernalia, such as dildos, whips, chains, bondage material and other like articles;

6. Photographs, video cassettes and any printed material depicting obscene matter as defined in Penal Code section 101(a-q);

7. Personal effects, including purses, wallets, handbags and other like articles;

8. Tape recorders and other recording devices, specifically answering machines, and tapes for tape recorders and other sound devices;

9. Any and all "Trick Bags," which normally consist of cloth bags or other containers, sometimes including a woman's large handbag, which will generally enclose the following items which are used in the practice of prostitution: clothing, especially a change of undergarments such as panties, bras, camisoles, and negligees, wet wipes, paper tissues, Vaseline and personal lubricants, bottles of mouth wash, rubbing alcohol, baby oil, various kinds and numbers of condoms, douches and other forms of feminine hygiene, and various cosmetics, small hand towels which are normally used in the practice of prostitution to wipe the ejaculatory excretions from the bodies of the prostitute and the customers, books, magazines, and any other publications or pictures of individuals and/or beasts of the same or opposite sex in various sexual positions and/or acts;

10. To listen to, note and record any messages left on any telephone answering devices and/or machines and/or pagers inside the location, and to answer any incoming phone calls during the service of this search warrant;

11. Indicia of occupancy or ownership; articles of personal property tending to establish the identity of persons in control of the said premises, storage areas or containers where the above items are found consisting of rent receipts, cancelled checks, telephone records, utility company records, charge card receipts, cancelled mail, keys and warranties;

12. All incoming phone calls; searching officers are directed to search by answering the telephone and conversing with callers who appear to be calling in regard to massages, sensual massages, therapeutic massages, full-body massages, prostate massages, complete massages or acts of prostitution, and noting and recording the conversation without revealing their true identity; and

13. Articles of personal property tending to establish the identity of persons in control of the premises being searched, such as utility company receipts, rent receipts, charge card receipts, tax receipts, checks, deposit slips, savings account passbooks, passports, driver's licenses, vehicle registration/titles, land titles, escrow papers, legal documents, Social Security cards, insurance bills and/or policies, medical records, prescriptions and prescription bottles, doctor bills, hospital bills, cancelled mail, addressed envelopes, photographs, keys and safes.

And if you find the same or any part thereof, to bring it forthwith before me or this court, or any other court in which the said offense in respect to which the property or things taken is triable, or retain such property in your custody, subject to the order of this court pursuant to Penal Code section 1066.

4/1/03   1:45 pm.
_____
Date/Time

_R. Beam_____
Signature of Magistrate

ENDORSEMENT FOR NIGHT SERVICE

For good cause I direct that this warrant be served at any time of the day or night.

_____
Endorsement of Magistrate

(Seal) P.C. 1719, 2329, 3137, 4143, 4751, 5357, 5961

1 COMMONWEALTH OF EAST CAROLINA, COUNTY OF GOTHAM

2 **SEARCH WARRANT**

3

4   PEOPLE OF THE COMMONWEALTH OF EAST CAROLINA to any sheriff, policeman

5 or peace officer in the County of Gotham:

6 PROOF, by affidavit, having been made before me by

7   Officer Joseph Friendly   that there is probable cause to believe that the
       (name of affiant)

8 property described herein may be found at the locations set forth herein and

9 that it is seizable pursuant to Criminal Code §1939. You are therefore

10 COMMANDED to SEARCH

11   (1) The premises at 1001 Sales Ave., Apartment 62, Gotham City, further

12   described as an apartment unit within a six-story multi-unit apartment

13   building bearing the name "Regency Apartments," and all rooms, attics,

14   and other parts within Apartment 62, and all garages, trash

15   containers, and storage areas designated for the use of Apartment 62,

16   and

17   (2) The person of Christal Smith, further described as a female African-

18   American, 5 feet 6 inches, 130 pounds, short black hair, brown eyes,

19   approximately 25 years of age, and

20   (3) The vehicle described as a black 2003 Mercedes AMG, license plate

21   24OPEN7.

22 For the following property: amphetamines; drug paraphernalia consisting in

23 part of and including, but not limited to, baggies, aluminum foil wrapping,

24 scales and measuring spoons, and articles of personal property tending to

25 establish the identity of persons in control of the premises being searched

SEARCH WARRANT   1

including, but not limited to, utility company receipts, rent receipts,

addressed envelopes, and keys.

And to SEIZE it if found and bring it forthwith before me, or this court, at

the courthouse of this court.

GIVEN under my hand and dated

This _1_ day of ___April___, 2003

at _1:30_ a.m.
~~(p.m.)~~

Roy Bean
Signature of Magistrate

Judge of the ___Sup.___ Court ___Gotham___
Superior/Municipal   Judicial District

NIGHTTIME SERVICE ENDORSEMENT*

GOOD CAUSE HAVING BEEN SHOWN BY AFFIDAVIT, THIS WARRANT CAN BE SERVED AT ANY

TIMJE OF THE DAY OR NIGHT.

Roy Bean
Endorsement of Magistrate
for Nighttime Service

*Unless endorsed for nighttime service, this warrant can be served only
between 7:00 a.m. and 10:00 p.m.

SEARCH WARRANT   2

UNITED STATES DISTRICT COURT
DISTRICT OF NEW AMSTERDAM

In the Matter of the Search of

(name, address or brief description of person or property to be searched)   **SEARCH WARRANT**

210 East 13th St.
Lowerman, NA 20535   **CASE NO.** 24601

TO: Officers and Agents of the Federal Bureau of Investigation and all other authorized officers

Affidavit(s) having been made before me by <u>Special Agent Joseph Friendly</u>, who has reason to believe that ☐ on the person or ☒ on the property or premises known as

210 East 13th St.
Lowerman, NA 20535

In the District of New Amsterdam, there will be property, (describe the person or property)

See Attachment A

I am satisfied that the affidavits and any recorded testimony establish probable cause to believe that the property so described is now concealed on the premises above-described and establish grounds for the issuance of this warrant.

YOU ARE HEREBY COMMANDED to search on or before ____4/7/03_____
                                                                                     Date

(not to exceed 10 days) the person or place named above for the person or property specified, serving this warrant and making the search (in the daytime – 6:00 A.M. to 10:00 P.M.) and if the person or property be found there to seize same, leaving a copy of this warrant and receipt for the person or property taken, and prepare a written inventory of the person or property seized and promptly return this warrant to the Honorable Roy Bean, U.S. Magistrate Judge, as required by law.

___4/1/03___, at ___2:00 P.M.___, New Amsterdam
Date Issued

Roy Bean
Honorable Roy Bean
United States Magistrate Judge

Attachment A

Electronic data processing and storage devices, computers and computer systems, such as processing units, internal and peripheral storage devices such as fixed disks, external hard disks, floppy disks and drives, tape drives and media, optical storage or memory storage devices, peripheral input and output devices such as keyboards, mouses, printers, video display monitors, optical readers, and related communication devices such as acoustic or electrical modems, associated telephone sets, speed dialers, or other controlling devices, plotters, software to run programs, connecting cables and plugs, peripherals such as joysticks, mouses or other input devices, scanners, writing pads, manuals, power back up devices, connecting switches, power sources, telephones, cables and interface devices.

SUPERIOR COURT OF SOUTH VIRGINIA
SEARCH WARRANT

TO: _____ CHIEF OF POLICE OR ANY OTHER LAW ENFORCEMENT OFFICER _____
(Specific Law Enforcement Officer or Classification of Officer of the Iskandaria Police Department or other Authorized Agency)

AFFIDAVIT, herewith attached, having been made before me by <u>Joseph Friendly Badge 1054</u> that he has probable cause to believe that on the <u>premises</u> known as <u>1812 Commencement Blvd., Iskandaria, SV 20535</u> as described more fully in the Affidavit in Support of a South Virginia Superior Court Search Warrant which is incorporated herein by reference, there is now being concealed property, namely <u>firearm(s) and the following properties associated with firearms; ammunition, holsters, gun cleaning kits, pawn slips regarding such firearms, registration slips regarding said firearms and indicia showing ownership of such firearms;</u>

YOU ARE HEREBY AUTHORIZED within 10 days of the date of issuance of this warrant to search in the <u>(daytime)</u> at any time of the day or night, the designated <u>premises</u> for the property specified, and if the property be found there

YOU ARE COMMANDED TO SEIZE IT, TO WRITE AND SUBSCRIBE in an inventory of the property seized, to leave a copy of this warrant and return, and to file a further copy of this warrant and return with the Court on the next court day after its execution.

Issued this __1__ day of __April__, 20_03_   _Roy Bean_____
Judge, Superior Court of South Virginia

RETURN

I received the above warrant on ____4/1____, 20_03_ and have executed it as follows: On ___4/2___, 20_03_ at _5:30 P._ M., I searched the <u>premises</u> described in the warrant and I left a copy of the warrant and return with _____CHRISTOPHER SMITH_____ properly posted.
(name of person searched or owner, occupant, custodian or person present at place of search)

The following is an inventory of the property taken pursuant to this warrant:

1- NORINCO ASSAULT RIFLE

1- ENFIELD ASSAULT RIFLE LOADED W/ HOLLOW POINT BULLETS

1- BOX CARBON 38 CAL. BULLETS

2- BOXES 44 CAL. BULLETS

1- BOX PMC 45 CAL. BULLETS

1- NIGHT VISION SCOPE

1- GUN CLEANING KIT

ASSORTED GUN MAGAZINES, WEAPONS CATALOGS, NRA LITERATURE

This inventory was made in the presence of _CHRISTOPHER SMITH_____

I swear that this is a true and detailed account of all property taken by me under this warrant.

_J. Friendly_____
Executing Officer

Subscribed and sworn to before me this __3rd__ day of __April_____, 20_03_

_Roy Bean_____
Judge, Superior Court of South Virginia

Form CD(17)-1055/Mar.89

8

WARRANTLESS SEARCHES

SEARCHES BASED ON CONSENT

Law enforcement officers can search without a warrant under a wide variety of circumstances. Among these, there's only one situation in which you have any chance of preventing the intrusion—and that's by saying "I don't consent" when the police ask whether they can search. This is a powerful tool for using your civil rights, as important as remaining silent and asking to see a lawyer.

The right that upholds your privacy is the Fourth Amendment to the U.S. Constitution, which protects your body, home, papers and possessions from unreasonable searches and seizures. Law enforcement agents are forbidden to violate your privacy unless they have a specific legal justification, such as executing a valid warrant or following a fleeing suspect in hot pursuit. If officers are asking your permission to search, that means that they don't honestly believe they have one of these lawful excuses—so they're hoping that you'll foolishly give up your rights and consent to the search.

An officer's request to search often sounds like an informal order, as in:

> *Why don't you show me what you've got in that bag?*

> *There's been a report of an incident near here. I want to come in and take a look around.*

> *Let's see some i.d.*

The officer won't point out that you have the option to refuse. So it's up to you not to open or unpack anything, until you've verified that the police are giving you an actual order. You can say, "Are you just asking me, or are you ordering me?" Either the cop will give up, or he'll specifically order you to comply with the search.

Obviously, if the officer just leaves you alone, you're in good shape. And even if the officer insists on searching over your objection and finds something incriminating, you'll have prevented the prosecutor from arguing that you consented to the search—which gives your lawyer a better chance of getting the evidence suppressed, on the grounds that it may have been seized illegally.

When the police imply that you're hiding something, remember that you don't have anything to prove. If the police are asking permission to search, that means *you're* in the position of power. To use it, all you have to do is say, "I don't consent."

Saying "I don't consent" may seem a little formal, but it helps keep the police from claiming that they thought you gave them permission. Many cases have been lost because the defendant was too polite or intimidated to refuse consent clearly. For example, if you said, "I'd rather you didn't come in," it could be argued that you were permitting the officers to enter your home, while just expressing a little discomfort about it.

Law enforcement agents may try to invite themselves into your house, even though they don't have a valid legal reason for entering. However, the right to privacy in your own home is very strong,[1] provided that you stay alert and say "I don't consent" when the police ask to come in.[2] It's even easier to do this if you keep the door closed while you refuse to give them permission:

The police will often tell you they don't need a warrant to come into your house, because they have a legal rationale such as probable cause. That may or may not be true. But it's always safest to reply: "I don't consent to your coming in." This statement cannot harm you, and it will be helpful in court if the police are wrong or lying.

If the police insist on coming in after you've refused consent, stand back and let them through the door—but remind them, even as you're stepping aside, that you still don't consent to their entering. Do not physically resist the police when refusing consent, because you're likely to get hurt and charged with obstructing or assaulting an officer.

Sometimes, the police will threaten you or bargain with you, to get you to consent to a search of your home. For example, the officer may say, "Look, if I have to go back downtown and get a warrant, I am not going to be happy. And if that happens, by the time I get through searching, this place is going to look like a hurricane hit it." This isn't meaningful, because the police normally

trash your house anyway when they search. You can expect your home to be "tore up from the floor up," so you might as well refuse consent and see whether the officer can actually obtain a warrant.

What's really scary is when the police threaten to take your kids or pets away, if you don't consent to a search. The less-subtle threats sound like this:

- *You want to do this the easy way, and just let us in? Or you want to do it the hard way—we go get a warrant and while we're at it, we call Child Protective Services?*

- *That's a nice little dog you got there. Why don't we come in and do a walk-through, to make sure everything's okay? Or, we can go get a warrant. Then we'll come back, bust you, and send your dog to the pound. You might get out of jail before they put him to sleep, or then again you might not...*

Whatever the threat is, you shouldn't consent to let them in. If the police don't come back, then they couldn't really get a warrant and you'll have called their bluff. If the police do come back, you'll at least have had time to call friends or family to come get your children or pets. And you'll have been able to call a lawyer for advice or help during the search.

It's critical that all the people who live in your home, including temporary houseguests, understand that they must not consent to let the police enter or search. (Your door chain is only as strong as its weakest link.) The police can rely on consent from anyone who appears to be a resident or lawful user of the property. So you have a real problem if the person who answers the door is just a friend who came to dinner, who doesn't know to say, "I don't consent." One way to prevent accidents is to post instructions inside, on or near the door, stating:

> Dear Guests:
>
> We do not consent to have law enforcement officers enter or search our home. We do not authorize anyone else to consent on our behalf. If an officer asks to come in, say: "I don't consent."
>
> Thank you,
> [The Residents]

---

1. The Bill of Rights was written after the American Revolution, by people who personally remembered abuses of power by the British government, particularly the searches conducted by revenue officers. These officers were issued a kind of all-purpose search warrant, called a "writ of assistance," that allowed them to search wherever and whenever they wanted to. The Fourth Amendment was designed to prevent this from happening again—but it's not much good if you forget and give consent to search.

2. You'll have noticed that vampires can't cross your threshold either, unless you invite them.

Officers can even receive consent to enter your home from school-age children, so it's important to teach the kids, too, about their Fourth Amendment rights and the policy of your household.

If you're a tenant, your landlord is not entitled to let the police enter your home without a warrant, *unless* there's a provision in your lease authorizing the landlord to do so. So, if you rent, check your lease. Look for a sentence or two that says something like:

> Landlord reserves the right to allow entry of law enforcement officials, upon request.

– or –

> Landlord may admit law enforcement personnel onto premises, as needed, to further investigation or prevention of illegal activities.

Such clauses allow your landlord to consent to officers' entering your home, whether you agree or not.

OTHER TYPES OF WARRANTLESS SEARCHES

The following are some of the situations in which law enforcement agents can search without a warrant. But never just agree to a search because it appears that one of these reasons applies: make sure that the officer gives you a direct order, so it can't be argued that you consented to the search.

Court Supervision

A typical condition of court supervision (probation, parole, supervised release) is that law enforcement agents are allowed to search your person, vehicle, home, and/or workplace without probable cause (see Searches While Under Supervision, page 74).

Search Following Arrest

When you're arrested, the officers can search your body and the belongings you have with you. If you're indoors, the officers can search the area under your immediate control (the distance to which you can lunge). Officers can have blood samples or fingernail scrapings taken, to preserve potential evidence that would otherwise disappear.

Automobile Searches

If you're arrested in a car, the officers can search the passenger compartment, because that's the area under your immediate control. Whether or not anyone's been arrested, if law enforcement agents have probable cause[3] to believe that your vehicle contains proof of a crime, they can search it without a warrant—and open any container in the car that might hold the items they're seeking. If your car is impounded for any reason, even for just being in a tow-away zone, the officers can search the whole vehicle, including the trunk.

Exigent Circumstances

"Exigent," in this context, means urgent, a circumstance that demands immediate attention. Law enforcement agents can enter when there's a fire or other danger, to deal with it or to rescue people, and they can investigate the cause of a fire for a limited time. In addition, officers can enter in hot pursuit of a serious criminal, or to capture one who's about to escape. Judges usually find that if the police had less than half an hour in which to act, then proceeding without a warrant is reasonable.

Emergency Response

When officers hear a cry for help, they can enter a building in response. If law enforcement agents believe that a child is being abused or is in other immediate danger, they can enter the premises to rescue her.

Students at Public Schools

On school grounds, school officials can search a student and the belongings she's carrying, if they have "reasonable suspicion" that the student has violated the law or a school rule. Reasonable suspicion is a lower standard than probable cause.[4]

The U.S. Supreme Court hasn't yet analyzed whether a student has a right to privacy in her locker or desk. Various lower courts have produced conflicting opinions. Under the circumstances, a sensible student would not want to keep her most private possessions at school.

Drug Testing

The courts sometimes find drug testing constitutional. High school students can be required to submit to random drug testing in order to engage in sports, band,

---

3. and 4. Probable cause is the amount of proof required to get a search warrant or arrest someone. Reasonable suspicion is the amount of proof required to detain someone. See Detention, page 4, and Arrest, page 5.

chorus, or academic competitions. Employees in certain high-risk jobs can be required to drug test (such as railroad workers who've been in an accident or broken safety rules; or applicants for U.S. Customs jobs that relate to drug-smuggling or that involve carrying a gun).

Airline Passengers

Passengers on airlines can be required to go through metal detectors and submit to searches of their bodies and their possessions, before boarding the plane. Of course, a passenger may change her mind and decide not to take the flight after all, in which case she can't be searched. However, once the passenger has cooperated with even part of the search process—by handing over her luggage or going through the metal detector—she cannot stop the process until the authorities are completely done searching.

SHOWING IDENTIFICATION

U.S. citizens do not have to carry identification with them.[5] Occasionally, cities or counties try to pass "anti-vagrancy" laws requiring everyone to carry identification, but such provisions have always been held unconstitutional when appealed to higher courts.

However, in order to drive most vehicles, you are required to have a license and to produce it on demand. For example, failure to have your driver's license with you while driving your car can result in a ticket or even arrest. When you're simply traveling, you may drive through other states relying on the license issued in your home state. But if you move to a different state, you'll have a limited amount of time (for example, 30 days) to get a driver's license for your new home state. If your license is suspended in a particular state, you can't drive in that state at all, no matter which other states' licenses you possess—it's your privilege to drive that's been cancelled, not just the piece of paper the state issued you.

SEARCHES AT OR NEAR THE NATIONAL BORDER

Law enforcement agents *at the border or screening passengers from an international plane flight* have the authority to question and search people who are entering the country (citizens and non-citizens alike) to a virtually unlimited extent.

Law enforcement agents can set up fixed checkpoints on roads inside the United States, but near to the border, and stop cars for questioning. The officers don't need any proof of wrongdoing to question the car's occupants, but to search the car they must have probable cause or consent.

Law enforcement agents can also drive around in the vicinity of the border and stop cars that the officers reasonably suspect contain people who've entered the country illegally. The officers can question the occupants of the car, but they can't search the vehicle—unless a rationale for a warrantless search applies.

---

5. There have been more frequent attempts lately, to pass laws that would issue each U.S. citizen a "national identification card" and/or require everyone to carry identification with them at all times. No such legislation is in effect, however, at the time of this writing (January, 2004).

9

SURVEILLANCE

Government surveillance can take many forms, some of which require a warrant or other court order, and some of which require no authorization whatsoever.[1]

VISUAL SURVEILLANCE

If you're in a place open to public view, you can be watched, photographed or videoed without notice or permission. This means that your picture can be taken while you're walking around town, driving through an intersection or sitting in a stadium. In fact, you don't necessarily have to be in a public place. If you're visible through a window, your image can be recorded even though you're inside your own house.

Law enforcement agents can also fly over your property in a plane or helicopter—even as low as 400 feet—looking for illegal activity such as marijuana cultivation. Naturally, they can take photos while they're at it.

Conversely, there can be private spots in public places. In a public toilet, you can't legally be watched or photographed while you're inside a stall with the door closed, because then you're not in the public view. Generally, when you're in a place where passersby can't see you—where you have a "reasonable expectation of privacy"[2]—the government is not entitled to observe you covertly.

Remember, though, that if you're given notice of potential surveillance, you lose your reasonable expectation of privacy. Examples of such notices are: "dressing rooms are monitored to deter shoplifting" or "these premises are protected by a closed circuit security system."

Video and photograph surveillance is used now to detect and record criminal activity. It will also be used in searching for particular individuals, as facial recognition technology becomes more effective.

SURVEILLANCE OF TELEPHONE COMMUNICATIONS

When you're speaking on the telephone, you have a reasonable expectation of privacy—unless there's someone standing near enough to overhear. To listen to your phone conversations secretly, law enforcement agents

need a wiretap warrant. Wiretap warrants have rather strict requirements. The officers:

1. must show probable cause that a specific crime has been or is being committed;

2. must list names of specific person(s) to be overheard;

3. must give detailed descriptions of subjects to be overheard;

4. must stop listening within 30 days (or seek a 30-day extension);

5. must include provisions for terminating the wiretap; and

6. must report to the judge concerning intercepted conversations.

Wiretap warrants are more trouble for the police to obtain and report on than regular search warrants, so they're less commonly used. By contrast, law enforcement agents frequently employ a "pen register" and/or "trap and trace device." A pen register is a list of the telephone numbers of *outgoing* calls from a particular phone line. A trap and trace device collects the phone numbers of *incoming* calls to a particular line. Both types of surveillance collect the time and length of the calls, as well. To utilize a pen register or trap and trace device, the police just need a court order, which they get by showing that the information derived would be relevant to an ongoing criminal investigation.

For an important case, the officers will still want a wiretap, since it reveals the actual conversations, while a pen register or trap and trace device just provides a list of phone numbers.

Note that law enforcement agents can obtain voice mail with a regular search warrant—they don't need a wiretap warrant. Many people prefer to use an answering machine, rather than a voice mail service, because it provides more control over the privacy of stored messages.

There are two situations in which investigating officers can legally listen to and record your phone conversations without getting a wiretap warrant.

- calls from a prisoner in a jail, prison or immigration detention facility (including calls from a prisoner to a lawyer)

---

1. As with most areas of law, the rules concerning surveillance vary to some degree from state to state. This chapter discusses federal law, which in the context of surveillance constitutes the minimum standard of privacy protection (such as it is). For detailed, up-to-date information on state and federal government surveillance, among other topics, see the Electronic Frontier Foundation's website: http://eff.org/.

2. "Reasonable expectation of privacy" is a phrase that comes up a lot in legal arguments involving searches and seizures. It relates to the rights provided by the Fourth Amendment to the U.S. Constitution. See Searches Based on Consent, page 106.

- calls to or from an undercover officer or an informant.

Sometimes, while on the phone, people speculate or make jokes about the line being tapped. This is a poor idea, since acknowledging that someone may be listening means that you *don't* have a reasonable expectation of privacy. If you're on the phone and someone does make a stupid comment about the line being tapped, say: "That's a silly joke. I believe that I have a reasonable expectation of privacy in this phone conversation."

There are certainly instances in which law enforcement agents listen to phone conversations illegally. Such unlawful activities may not come to light if the officers are clever in laundering the information they've obtained, for example, attributing it to a confidential informant. It's easier for law enforcement to listen illegally to a cordless phone or a cell phone, than to a corded phone (the kind that has a curly cord running from the receiver to the phone itself).[3]

SURVEILLANCE OF MAIL

Mail cannot be opened without probable cause, but no authorization is needed for mail to be sniffed by law enforcement dogs trained to seek drugs or other contraband.

Mail sent or received across the national border can be opened and searched, if there is "reasonable cause" to suspect that it contains contraband, however, the officers are not supposed to read any accompanying correspondence.

Mail sent to or from a prisoner in a jail, prison or immigration detention center, can be opened and read by the authorities. Letters to or from a prisoner's lawyer can be opened and shaken out, but not read. However, it's important to verify with the particular facility exactly how to label the envelope, to make sure it will be treated as confidential legal mail. For example, one institution may want you to write "attorney/client correspondence," while another may tell you to put "legal mail—privileged and confidential."

SURVEILLANCE OF GARBAGE

Once you put your trash out to be picked up, on the curb or in a dumpster, you're considered to have abandoned any claim to it. So, since it's no longer your property, it's not protected by the Fourth Amendment. You might consider using more thorough methods of disposal, such as incineration, when privacy is particularly important.

SURVEILLANCE OF INTERNET ACTIVITY

The Internet is an efficient, but not particularly private, method of communication.

To begin with, whatever you say in a chat room or IRC channel is necessarily a public statement—you don't have a reasonable expectation of privacy in this context. Using a nickname or handle doesn't guarantee that you're anonymous—such identifiers can generally be traced to their owners.

In addition, your Internet Service Provider (ISP) may have already put you on notice in their "Terms of Service" that, under certain circumstances, they'll voluntarily disclose "content"—not just illegal content, but also material that may only be "vulgar" or "otherwise objectionable." And with a simple subpoena, the government can obtain the content of users' communications as well as information about users, including addresses and financial data (such as credit card or bank account numbers).

There has been an increasing amount of litigation and legislation concerning Internet privacy. For example, the USA PATRIOT Act[4] allows law enforcement agencies to monitor Internet usage and communications to a high degree.

The USA PATRIOT Act extends the idea of pen registers and trap and trace devices to email. With an easily obtained court order, law enforcement can gather the addresses and routing information that are part of every email message. Yet there's a big difference between phone calls and email. It's easy to track phone numbers without listening to the content of phone conversations; but it's hard to separate addresses and routing from the content of the email messages, because the information is packaged and transmitted together.

---

3. Although many telephones are advertised as being particularly secure against eavesdropping, surveillance technology is improving all the time. The system that ensures privacy today may not do so tomorrow. In the end, the most private conversations are those conducted while walking around outdoors—assuming the person you're talking to isn't an undercover officer or an informant.

4. The USA PATRIOT Act (Uniting and Strengthening Americans by Providing Appropriate Tools Required to Intercept and Obstruct Terrorism Act of 2001) was made law on 10/26/01.

With somewhat more effort, the government can also get a wire-tap warrant for your email, which lays bare all aspects of your electronic communications.

The USA PATRIOT Act allows law enforcement agents to monitor "non-content"[5] web surfing, as long as they get a court order (for which they only need to state that the information is relevant to an ongoing criminal investigation). And the USA PATRIOT Act permits ISPs to give the government all "non-content" information about your online communications

To keep the content of your electronic communications private, encrypt them with PGP Mail. PGP stands for Pretty Good Privacy, and it's been proven strong enough to deter government attempts to penetrate your email. To get the latest version of PGP Mail (either the complete version[6] or the freeware version), go to http://www.philzimmermann.com/. (Note that Zimmermann ends with two n's.)

5. The USA PATRIOT Act refers to "non-content" material, but this term has not yet been defined.

6. The complete version comes with PGP Disk, an application that encrypts data on your computer and your storage media—an excellent idea!

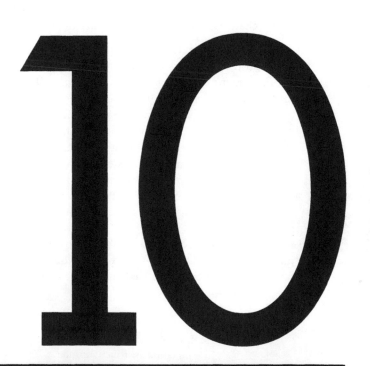

10

GRAND JURIES

WHAT A GRAND JURY DOES

Grand juries are one of the good intentions paving the road to our current legal system. Unlike a trial jury, which decides whether a suspect is guilty, a grand jury merely decides whether there's probable cause to prosecute a suspect on felony charges. The goal was to create a filter to catch unjustified felony cases and stop them at an early stage, so that the suspect wouldn't be wrongfully prosecuted (and have to spend unnecessary time in jail and unnecessary money on lawyers).[1] But it all went very wrong.

Grand juries are generally composed of six to twenty-three members, depending on the jurisdiction. In the federal system and in most states, grand jurors serve for eighteen months and judge many different cases (but they usually meet just once a week or even once a month). At a grand jury hearing, the only official is the prosecutor—there's no judge and no defense attorney. The jurors sit there listening to witnesses and reviewing exhibits in a prospective or pending felony case, and then vote on whom to prosecute.[2] Once the grand jury decides there's probable cause, the prosecutor can issue an indictment (ĭn-dīt´mənt), a document specifying the felony charge(s) against a particular defendant.

The prosecutor selects all the witnesses and other materials, and then presents them to the grand jury. Defense attorneys aren't even allowed in same room as the grand jury, let alone permitted to put on defense witnesses, question the prosecution witnesses, or make any statements to the jurors. So grand juries nearly always just "rubber stamp" the cases brought before them. For example, in fiscal year 2000, federal grand juries voted to indict a total of 59,472 suspects[3] and chose not to indict 29 suspects[4]—only one out of every two thousand suspects was left un-indicted. An additional factor in grand juries' unwholesome compliance with prosecutorial plans is the frequent lack of diversity among the jurors. Occasionally—but not often enough—this is brought to light by a case challenging the constitutionality of a grand jury that doesn't reflect the demographics of its county or federal district.[5]

Some people who are called as witnesses at grand jury hearings, are prosecuted afterward. If you're ordered to appear before a grand jury, immediately seek the advice of an attorney who has experience in grand jury matters. Unfortunately, as a grand jury witness, you're not entitled to a court-appointed attorney, even if you're low-income. Nonetheless, it's really important to get a lawyer: you don't want to gamble when the stakes are this high and the game is rigged.

BEING SERVED WITH A SUBPOENA

A subpoena[6] (sə-pēn´ə) is an order requiring you to be present at a legal proceeding, such as a trial or a grand jury hearing. (See sample grand jury subpoena, page 118.) Usually you're summoned just to testify, but sometimes you're required to bring documents or other items with you. A subpoena with an order that you bring something is a subpoena duces tecum (dū´səs tāk´oom).[7] If you don't appear when you're told (bringing any specified items), a judge can have you taken into custody and brought to the hearing from jail.

Once in a great while, a lawyer may be able to persuade a judge to "quash" a grand jury subpoena, but the subpoenas are nearly always upheld.

A subpoena must be served on you before you're bound by it. Normally, grand jury subpoenas are delivered to you, in person, by a law enforcement officer, who can come and find you at your home, work, school, etc.

APPEARING BEFORE A GRAND JURY

Although your lawyer can't accompany you into the grand jury room, she can wait outside the door, ready to advise you. A grand jury witness is legally entitled to get legal advice before answering each and every question. For example, a person can write down the first question

---

1. Grand juries are mandated by the Fifth Amendment to the U.S. Constitution, which also includes protection against self-incrimination, the right to due process, and other eroded liberties.

2. There are "special grand juries" that actively investigate crime or corruption, but these are rarely instituted, compared to regular grand juries.

3. Sourcebook of criminal justice statistics Online, "Grand jury and grand juror utilization in U.S. District Courts," Table 1.74, http://www.albany.edu/sourcebook/1995/pdf/t174.pdf (accessed October 16, 2003).

4. Bureau of Justice Statistics, U.S. Department of Justice, Compendium of Federal Justice Statistics, 2000, "Basis for declination of prosecution by U.S. Attorneys," Table 2.4, 30, http://www.ojp.usdoj.gov/bjs/pub/pdf/cfjs0002.pdf (accessed October 16, 2003).

5. Racially biased grand juries are sufficiently frequent and widespread that in 1977, the U.S. Supreme Court set forth specific grounds for determining whether a grand jury has been improperly composed (Castaneda v. Partida, 430 U.S. 482 (1977)).

6. Subpoena is a Medieval Latin word combining sub (under) + poena (penalty); that is, "under penalty of law."

7. More Latin: duces (you must bring) tecum (with you).

as soon as it's asked, leave the room and talk to his lawyer, and then go back into the hearing room and give his response to that question. Then he would listen to the *next* question, write it down, go out and talk to his lawyer, and come back to give his response. Then he would write down the *third* question, go talk to his lawyer, and so on...

Once you're in front of a grand jury, you can testify or you can "take the Fifth" (exercise your right to remain silent).

If you decide to testify, don't expect to get away with evading any of the questions or saying, "I can't remember" over and over. The person doing the questioning will be a prosecutor who's used to squeezing details out of reluctant witnesses.

If you do take the Fifth, you won't have to say so more than a few times. Once you've exercised your right to remain silent in response to several questions, and it's clear that you're not going to give any further answers, you'll be excused. However, there's a hitch. Sometimes, the prosecutor grants immunity to a witness who's exercising her right to remain silent, to try to force her to testify. It doesn't matter whether or not you've requested immunity. The prosecutor or judge can just impose immunity on you—and then you're no longer entitled to the protection of the Fifth Amendment (because if you're immune, what you say can't be used against you).

However, there are two kinds of immunity. The good kind is called "transactional immunity" and it means that you can't be prosecuted for the incident(s) you testify about. The bad kind is "use immunity" and it means that the prosecutor can't use your *own* testimony against you—but he can use *other people's* testimony and evidence against you. So if the prosecutor makes a bunch of people testify, they'll likely end up providing enough evidence to convict each other. Naturally, grand jury witnesses are almost always given use immunity, not transactional immunity.

If you refuse to testify after being granted immunity, you'll normally be held in contempt and locked up. Some people who've chosen not to comply have had to stay in custody until all the grand jury proceedings were ended or the case was over. This can take months or even years.

Since their inception, both in England and in the United States, grand juries have been used against political dissidents, the jurors often being hand-picked to ensure indictment. A modern variation on this abuse of power relies on political activists' reluctance to inform on their comrades. Activists are subpoenaed with the expectation that they will refuse to testify, and thus end up in jail for lengthy periods (thereby immobilizing that activist and deterring others).[8]

---

8. For a comprehensive, yet stirring, article on the history and corruption of grand juries, see Michael Deutsch, *The Improper Use of the Federal Grand Jury: An Instrument for the Internment of Political Activists*, 75 Journal of Criminal Law & Criminology 1159 (1984); also posted on the Just Cause Law Collective website: http://www.lawcollective.org/.

AD 110 (Rev. 12/89) Subpoena to Testify Before Grand Jury   GJ# 03-1 (ED-SV)

United States District Court

_____Eastern_____ DISTRICT OF _____South Virginia_____

TO: Christine Smith

**SUBPOENA TO TESTIFY
BEFORE GRAND JURY**

SUBPOENA FOR:

[X] PERSON   [X] DOCUMENT(S) OR OBJECT(S)

   YOU ARE COMMANDED to appear and testify before the Grand Jury of the United States District Court
at the place, date, and time specified below.

PLACE	COURTROOM
UNITED STATE DISTRICT COURT 401 Courthouse Square Iskandaria, South Virginia 20500	GRAND JURY ROOM
	DATE AND TIME 4/1/03 9:30 A.M.

YOU ARE ALSO COMMANDED to bring with you the following document(s) or object(s):

   See attachment.

☐ Please see additional information on reverse

   This subpoena shall remain in effect until you are granted leave to depart by the court or by an officer acting
on behalf of the court.

MAGISTRATE JUDGE OR CLERK OF COURT	DATE
BARTLEBY T. SCRIVENER, CLERK OF THE COURT	
(By) Deputy Clerk *B.F. Scrivener*	March 15, 2003

This subpoena is issued on application of the United Sates of America I. JAVERT UNITED STATES ATTORNEY	ATTORNEY'S NAME, ADDRESS and PHONE NUMBER I. JAVERT 400 Courthouse Square Iskandaria, South Virginia 20500 (202) 456-1111

ATTACHMENT

You are hereby required to bring with you and produce the following documents and things referring or relating to protest activities or preparation for protest activities on March 20 and 21, 2003. These documents and things should include, but not be limited to, the following:

1. Any and all hardcopy or electronic letters, notes, email, or other correspondence referring or relating to protest activities or preparation for protest activities on March 20 and 21, 2003.

2. Any and all photographs, videotapes, audiotapes, voice messages, or other recordings referring or relating to protest activities or preparation for protest activities on March 20 and 21, 2003.

3. Any and all hardcopy or electronic diaries, journals, calendars, appointment books, address books, or address lists used at any time after January 1, 2002.

4. Any and all agendas, notes, or attendance lists from meetings referring or relating to protest activities or preparation for protest activities on March 20 and 21, 2003.

5. Any and all organizational staff lists, membership lists, mailing lists, email lists, telephone trees, or schedules used at any time after January 1, 2002.

6. Any and all personal or organizational budgets, financial records, bank statements, credit card bills, receipts, pay stubs, or records of donations after January 1, 2002.

7. Any and all fundraising letters or other correspondence relating to fundraising, grant applications or grants, or lists of individual or institutional donors after January 1, 2002.

8. Any and all posters, handbooks, handouts, leaflets, postcards, or other printed material referring or relating to protest activities or preparation for protest activities on March 20 and 21, 2003.

9. Any and all banners, signs, armbands, costumes, masks, puppets, or other props relating to protest activities or preparation for protest activities on March 20 and 21, 2003.

11

RIGHTS OF MINORS

For purposes of criminal law, the age at which you cease to be a minor varies by state, from sixteen to nineteen. In most states, it's eighteen.[1]

THE RIGHTS OF MINORS TO REMAIN SILENT AND SEE A LAWYER

Minors who've been arrested have the rights to remain silent and to have a lawyer present during questioning. Law enforcement agents rather frequently say, "You're just a kid—you don't have any rights," or "You're under-age, the Constitution doesn't apply to you." These are lies, meant to intimidate you. So if you've been arrested, don't lose your nerve—just stick to the Magic Words: *I'm going to remain silent. I would like to see a lawyer.*

Many adults believe they have the right to require a minor to answer questions. They're wrong.

- Police and probation officers don't have the legal right to order minors to answer questions.

- Teachers and school officials don't have the legal right to order a student to answer questions.

- Parents don't have the legal right to order their kid to answer questions.

If you're a kid in trouble and adults are pushing you to answer questions, say nothing but: *I'm going to remain silent. I would like to see a lawyer.* (It's a form of resisting authority that will actually have good consequences, from a legal standpoint.)

Minors, in some states, have the right to have a parent or guardian[2] present during questioning. If you're arrested as a minor, don't worry about figuring out for sure whether you have this right—just go ahead and ask to have your parent with you if you're going to be questioned. It can't do any harm, and it may prevent your being interrogated, or provide your lawyer with ammunition for fighting your case.

- Minors who are taken into custody should say: *I'm going to remain silent. I would like to see a lawyer. I want to have my mother/father/guardian present if I'm being questioned.*

Now, your parent or guardian may refuse to help you, and you can't force them to do so. However, it won't hurt to ask for them. The one thing to watch out for is that sometimes parents or guardians mistakenly pressure their kid to talk to the police, before consulting with a lawyer. Don't do it! If you're in trouble, make sure to talk to a criminal defense lawyer *before* you follow the "advice" of police, probation officers, teachers or parents. (See the story *My Lawyer Made Me Do It*, page 68, for an example of a parent who insists that her daughter make a confession, instead of remaining silent.)

If a minor's family is low-income, the judge will typically appoint a lawyer from the public defender's office to represent the minor for free. If the family does have the money to hire an attorney, but refuses to do so, the court will normally appoint the public defender and may then bill the family for legal fees.

THE RIGHT OF MINORS TO REFUSE CONSENT TO SEARCHES

As you would expect, minors have the right to refuse consent to searches, just like adults. Read Chapter 8, Warrantless Searches, carefully to see how to do this. Most adults find it psychologically challenging to refuse consent to officers who want to search—and it's even harder when you're a kid.

What's really important is that parents and guardians do *not* have the right to consent to a search of their kid's body or backpack. (This often comes as a big surprise to the adults.) Parents and guardians don't have the legal right to consent to a search of their kid's room either, if the kid has genuine control over the space—that is, if no one (including adults) is allowed to enter the room without the kid's permission. If you're a kid who can negotiate this degree of privacy with your family, you should put up a notice like this:

---

1. The ages at which you're eligible to drive, drink, smoke, vote, or register for Selective Service can't be used to predict the age of majority with respect to criminal law. Check with a criminal defense lawyer, so that you'll know the correct age for your particular state.

2. If you're a minor, make sure you know who your guardian is—and if there isn't one, ask that a guardian be selected. Get your own copy of the document that names your guardian, and keep it where you'll be able to find it in an emergency. (If a particular guardian hasn't been designated, one of your adult relatives will normally be given custody of you, if your parents aren't available.)

Obviously, you're supposed to put your own name on the sign. If you share a room and everyone agrees they want to be safe, write in the names of your roommates, and change "I" to "We" and "my" to "our." You can decorate the sign all you want, as long as it's easy to read the words. If you don't feel like making your own sign, there's a fill-in-the-blanks sign on page 124 that you can photocopy. It's important to keep the door closed, because an officer standing in the open doorway might be able to see potential evidence and seize it on the grounds that it was "in plain view."

Having the only key and keeping the door locked is important, too. In many court cases it's been decided that the person who possesses the key is the one who has true control over a given room or building.

However, even the best arrangements can fall through. If you're a kid and the adults you live with get sufficiently upset with you, they might suddenly decide that your room is really theirs (and they're just letting you live in it). In which case, they might tear down your sign or take away your key—and let the police into your room. Bearing this in mind, you should consider carefully what things you choose to keep in your room.

Also note that at school, you and your property are at greater risk of being legally searched. Don't store items in your locker or desk that you really want to keep private (see Students at Public Schools, page 108).

DIFFERENCES BETWEEN JUVENILE AND ADULT COURT

In most places, there are differences in terminology in juvenile court. For example:

Adult	Minor
Bail Hearing	Detention Hearing
Trial	Fact-Finding Hearing
Complaint or Indictment[3]	Petition
Defendant	Respondent
Verdict	Adjudication
Guilty	Delinquent or Involved

In addition, there are some really big differences in procedure. In a juvenile case, you normally don't get a jury. Instead, the judge alone decides both whether you've broken the law and what your punishment will be. Another difference is that bail is generally not allowed for minors. To get out of custody before adjudication, the minor will have to prove that she's neither a flight risk nor a danger to the community. (You can use the strategies listed in Preparing for a Bail Hearing, beginning on page 132.) Finally, the courtroom is usually closed to the general public (including the media) in a juvenile case.

Ironically, for smaller offenses, the consequences for minors may be worse than for adults. Minors tend to be placed on probation for longer periods than adults, and the conditions of their probation are usually more numerous and obnoxious, with additions such as curfews, getting adequate grades, behaving respectfully to parents, etc.[4] On the other hand, minors who are found delinquent in serious cases and incarcerated may be better off, since their sentences will typically end in their early twenties; whereas an adult might get life in prison.

Sometimes minors are tried in adult court, typically in cases involving very serious crimes such as rape or murder. This usually happens to somewhat older minors, aged thirteen to seventeen.

JUVENILE DELINQUENCY RECORDS

The rules about juvenile records vary from state to state (and from state court to federal court). Generally, a minor's delinquency record will not be disclosed to the general public—although it is available to the police or to prosecutors. *Do not expect that your juvenile record will automatically be sealed when you reach adulthood.* Typically, there's paperwork that has to be done to seal the record.

Remember that sealing a record is different from getting it expunged. Sealing means that the record exists, but can't normally be looked at by courts, employers, etc. Expunging means that the record is actually destroyed. For many types of offenses, the record can't be expunged until a lengthy waiting period has passed, if it can be expunged at all. Check with a local criminal defense attorney to find out what options are available to you in your particular situation.

---

3. The complaint or indictment is the document on which the charges against the defendant are specified.

4. The policy reason for this is that the courts have more interest in rehabilitating minors than adults, so they like to give themselves plenty of time and leverage to do it, hence lengthy probation with lots of conditions.

_____'s Room

(Your Name)

I do not consent to have law enforcement officers or anyone else enter or search my room.

I do not authorize anyone else to consent on my behalf.

_____
(Your Signature)

_____
(Date)

12

RIGHTS OF NON- U.S. CITIZENS

Immigration law changes frequently, the more so in the wake of increased concerns about "terrorism" within the United States. All non-U.S. citizens should take care to understand their particular immigration status and their rights, and update their knowledge on a regular basis.

An important development is the massive re-organization of the agencies that handle immigration matters, which occurred on March 1, 2003. At that time, the Immigration and Naturalization Service (INS) was abolished and its functions were taken over by the Department of Homeland Security (DHS). Within the DHS, there are several agencies that deal with immigration concerns. The Bureau of Citizenship and Immigration Services (CIS) handles applications for green cards, citizenship, and related matters. The Bureau of Immigration and Customs Enforcement (ICE), as well as the Bureau of Customs and Border Protection (CBP), investigate activities such as immigration violations and smuggling.[1]

If you're not a U.S. citizen, any discussion at all with a government official can have a profound effect on your immigration status. So it's critical that you review your rights and responsibilities before talking to anyone from a government agency, particularly the: CIS, ICE, CBP, FBI, DEA, police department, highway patrol, sheriff's department, or U.S. Marshall's service.

When a non-U.S. citizen is taken into custody by an immigration officer or other law enforcement agent, the officer is required to contact that person's consulate, and a consular official is entitled to visit the prisoner. The officer is also supposed to inform the arrested person of these rights. Since you cannot count on the officer's following these regulations, it's best to know your rights in advance and to make sure that you, your friends, or your family contact the consulate independently.

Non-U.S. citizens who've been arrested for a crime have the rights to remain silent and to have a lawyer present during questioning. These rights are based on the Fifth and Sixth Amendments to the U.S. Constitution and they protect everyone, citizens and non-citizens, adults and children. You have these rights even if you are "undocumented" or no longer have a valid visa.

Immigration and other law enforcement officers often try to intimidate non-U.S. citizens by saying "You're a foreigner, you don't have any rights," or "The Constitution only applies to citizens, not aliens." These are lies (or gross ignorance). So if you've been arrested, it's critical that you invoke your rights—especially the right to remain silent—regardless of what the officers are telling you.

GETTING LEGAL ASSISTANCE

If you are in custody, your consulate has the right to send a consular official to visit you, wherever you're being held. Of course, the consulate may not choose to do so, but you should request it. You, or someone helping you, should at least call your consulate. Among other services, your consulate may be able to refer you to a reliable local immigration lawyer. Sometimes, a consular official will mistakenly advise people to cooperate with the immigration or other law enforcement officers, and recommend answering all their questions without first talking to a lawyer. This is bad advice. Make sure you consult with an immigration attorney before answering any questions or signing any papers.

Don't choose a lawyer just because you've seen a lot of advertisements for him. (You see a lot of advertisements for Taco Bell, too, but if you have a choice, you go to a good taqueria.) Ask people in your community for recommendations about lawyers who've proven that they can do a good job. Also, make sure you're working with an actual lawyer. There are "immigration services" run by paralegals (non-lawyers), which offer to "help you with the paperwork"—but you can't count on them to handle genuine legal problems correctly. Immigration law is a particularly complicated and rapidly changing specialty. If you're going to spend money on an immigration issue, you might as well hire a licensed attorney—and these aren't necessarily more expensive. If you look around, you may be able to find a "public interest" law office or law clinic, run by good lawyers who are dedicated to helping low-income people. Sometimes these are affiliated with local law schools.

STRATEGIES FOR NON-U.S. CITIZENS ARRESTED BY IMMIGRATION AUTHORITIES

Immigration officers seek out and detain[2] non-citizens on a regular basis, often raiding workplaces and jails.

If you're a non-U.S. citizen taken into custody by immigration officers, you should say: *I'm going to remain silent. I would like to see a lawyer. I want to contact my consulate.*

---

1. Both ICE and CBP are under the authority of the Directorate of Border and Transportation Security (BTS), one of five directorates within DHS.

2. When the immigration authorities are keeping someone in custody, it's often referred to as "detention." This immigration detention can last for months or even years, as opposed to the detention discussed in the criminal law context, which rarely exceeds a few hours (see Detention, page 4).

- Don't say or write your name.
- Don't say or write your address.
- Don't say or write which country you're from.
- Don't say or write anything about your employment.
- Don't say or write anything about your family or friends.

Contact an immigration attorney (directly or through family or friends) and get advice before saying or signing anything. If you're in custody (police station, jail, detention center, etc.), be careful when you use the telephone—do not discuss your name, citizenship, or how you came to be arrested, because law enforcement agents are allowed to listen to prisoners' phone calls. You can't rely on speaking in your native language to maintain confidentiality, because many officers speak languages other than English, such as Spanish or Tagalog. When you telephone your attorney, you can identify yourself through the information on your wristband (the authorities normally put a plastic identification band on your wrist, if they're going to keep you in custody). If you've successfully withheld your name, your wristband will say "Jane Doe" or "John Doe," along with a number. So, for example, you might call your lawyer and say, "Hi, this John Doe 314159 at the Immigration Detention Center…"

The reason for maintaining this degree of privacy is that in order to expel you, the government must prove:

(1) your identity, and

(2) that you are not legally entitled to be in the United States.

Therefore, if you tell the immigration officers who you are, or give them enough information to figure it out, you've lost half the battle. And if you discuss your immigration status, you may have lost the battle entirely. Even if the immigration officers have *some* information, it would be unwise to give them any more, without consulting an immigration lawyer.

STRATEGIES FOR NON-U.S. CITIZENS ARRESTED BY LAW ENFORCEMENT AGENCIES

When law enforcement officers arrest people for criminal offenses, they're quick to turn over people they suspect of being non-citizens to the immigration authorities (especially people of color and those who speak English as a second language). Some jails even have an immigration agent permanently stationed there, to check the immigration status of every incoming prisoner.

Nonetheless, sometimes the police don't notice that an arrestee might not be a U.S. citizen. Therefore, if you're a non-U.S. citizen arrested by law enforcement agents *other than* immigration officers, your first important decision is whether or not to identify yourself.

If you're going to be given a promise to appear (see page 30) and released, then you should give your name and address.

or

If you're going to be kept in jail, you should withhold your name and address, because you stand a good chance of being turned over the immigration authorities.

The difficulty lies in determining whether you're really going to be given a promise to appear. Police often just pretend that they're going to release you on your promise to appear (see examples, page 56 and *Use a Pie, Go to Jail*, page 46). It's hard to know for certain until the officers actually hand you the paperwork and let you go.

Whether or not you give your name, you must still invoke your rights to remain silent and to have an attorney present before answering any questions. This applies whether you've been arrested by a police officer, sheriff, FBI agent, or any other type of law enforcement officer.

If you're a non-U.S. citizen taken into custody by the police, sheriffs, FBI, or any other law enforcement agents, you should say: *I'm going to remain silent. I would like to see a lawyer.*

Unless you're sure that the officers have already decided you're not a U.S. citizen, don't ask to contact your consulate. Have your friends or family contact your consulate, instead. There is no point in drawing the officers' attention to the issue of citizenship, if they aren't already considering it.

Non-U.S. citizens who have been charged with a crime have the same rights as U.S. citizens in criminal court, including:

- the right to remain silent
- the right to an attorney paid for by the court if the accused person is low-income
- the right to a trial (including a speedy trial)

Be aware that, in addition to or instead of the criminal case, non-U.S. citizens may have to face immigration proceedings. Some immigration proceedings are no more than a quick decision by a single immigration agent (see Voluntary Departure, Expedited Removal, etc., this page). The most formal proceeding is an immigration hearing, however these hearings are usually shorter than criminal trials and defendants have fewer rights in the process. In an immigration hearing, you are not entitled to a jury or a court-appointed lawyer (although you can hire a lawyer to represent you). The hearing takes place before an immigration judge, and the timing of the hearing depends on whether you are in or out of custody. Unfortunately, immigration judges are often cynical and biased against non-citizens. By law, less evidence is required for a judge to decide that someone has violated immigration laws, than for a judge or jury to decide that someone has broken criminal laws.

If you are considering a plea bargain in a criminal case, you *must* consult with an immigration attorney before deciding whether to accept the offer. Some deals that are fine for U.S. citizens are bad for foreign nationals. Sentences that seem very favorable in the context of the criminal case can still have disastrous results later on, if the immigration authorities take an interest. Consequences may include expulsion, denial of re-entry, or denial of naturalization.

ENTERING AND RE-ENTERING THE UNITED STATES

Non-U.S. citizens do not have the right to enter the United States, unless they are lawful permanent residents (people with green cards). And even green card holders cannot re-enter the United States if they have become "inadmissible." A valid visa does not guarantee entry, it simply entitles you to apply for admission to the United States.

If you have a criminal case pending, do not leave the United States without consulting an immigration attorney. You might be stopped at the border and denied re-entry, even though you have a green card or were attempting to come back for a hearing. There are remedies for this, but you should make the arrangements before you leave. Besides, under most circumstances, the conditions of your release will prohibit long-distance travel without special permission from the judge.

If you have just entered the United States (at the border or on an international plane flight), and immigration or customs officers want you to sign a document and then leave the country, be extremely careful. The document is likely to involve "voluntary departure" or, worse, some form of "removal." Demand to telephone an attorney for advice, before signing anything. Insist on getting a copy of any document you do sign.

VOLUNTARY DEPARTURE, EXPEDITED REMOVAL, REINSTATED REMOVAL, AND ADMINISTRATIVE REMOVAL

Voluntary departure and the various forms of removal (expedited, reinstated or administrative) are each quick-and-dirty procedures that the immigration authorities use for expelling a non-U.S. citizen. None of these processes involves an immigration hearing.

Voluntary departure means that you agree to leave the United States, without attempting to assert any rights to stay. Many people do so after being intimidated by immigration agents who have taken them into custody. Non-citizens should never agree to voluntary departure without first checking with an immigration lawyer to see whether that's really the best option. This may mean remaining in custody somewhat longer, but you must avoid panicking and giving up your rights simply because you've been detained by the authorities.

Expedited removal is a fast-track deportation procedure that can result in expulsion from the United States within a day or two. If you are assisting someone who has been detained, and you believe that the authorities are going to engage in expedited removal, you should (1) retain an immigration attorney immediately, and (2) have as many people as possible (preferably hundreds) contact the individual's consulate and urge the consular officials to become involved. It's also useful to have politicians and clergy visit the individual in custody. The point is to let the immigration authorities know that the case is under public scrutiny. Try to prevent the removal order from being issued in the first place. There are legal remedies once expedited removal has occurred, but the removal order must be appealed within 30 days!

Administrative removal is a procedure allowing the immigration authorities to expel a person who has been convicted of any of a wide variety of crimes, including many felonies and some misdemeanors. Typically, the convicted person will have served time in jail or prison and when the sentence is up, instead of being released, the prisoner is held until the immigration authorities pick him up and send him back to his country of origin. Administrative removal does not apply to lawful permanent residents (people with green cards).

Reinstated removal means that at some time in the past, you were expelled under an order for expedited or administrative removal, so now the immigration authorities can simply re-expel you. Once you have been subject to any kind of removal, you are tainted for all time. Removal can happen relatively unobtrusively at the border, so if you believe it's possible that you might ever have been removed, it would be wise to consult an immigration attorney to help you verify it.

IMMIGRATION CONSEQUENCES OF ARREST OR CONVICTION

The immigration consequences of arrest or conviction depend on your present immigration status, as well as on your race, class, and country of origin. Under many circumstances, the result is expulsion from the United States, often with a permanent or lengthy (five years) restriction on re-entry.

If you entered the United States without a visa or a visa waiver, your chances of being detained by the authorities and then sent home are high. You needn't have committed any other crime, since being in the country illegally is itself grounds for expulsion.

If you entered the United States legally, but your visa has expired, you are still at high risk of being expelled.

If you do not have a valid visa, be sure to ask your immigration lawyer whether you qualify for "political asylum" or other such programs. To qualify for asylum, you have to show that you would be in extreme danger if you were returned to your native country. There are also programs designed to help non-U.S. citizens who have been abused in the United States, such as victims of domestic violence, or people who have been forced to work against their will as domestic servants, prostitutes, or laborers.

If you entered the United States legally and your visa is still valid, then your immigration consequences depend on the type of visa, the outcome of the case, and the crime(s) of which you're convicted. If you are merely here on a temporary visa, your risk of expulsion is higher. If you are a lawful permanent resident (have a green card), you have more legal maneuvers available, but you could be still be expelled even though you may have lived in the United States most of your life.

If you are acquitted of the charge(s) against you, there is generally little impact on your immigration status. If you are convicted, then it is more likely that you will be expelled. (Note that if you are sentenced to incarceration, you will have to serve your time before you are sent out of the country.) There are three levels of crime, and convictions for the more serious crimes are obviously worse from an immigration standpoint.

If convicted of a felony (a crime punishable by prison time), the risk of being expelled is high, especially if the offense involves drugs, firearms, violence, sex or dishonesty (like fraud). During a felony case, you should make sure your criminal defense lawyer works closely with an immigration lawyer who's experienced in criminal issues.

If convicted of a misdemeanor (a crime punishable by a year in jail or less), the chances of being expelled are lower, but you're still at considerable risk if the offense involves drugs, firearms, violence, sex or dishonesty. Deliberately giving incorrect information to an officer (like a false address or false name) is only a misdemeanor, but it can have serious immigration consequences because the offense involves dishonesty. Remember that while it's illegal to give false information, it's okay to give *no* information. You always have the right to remain silent.

If you are convicted of an infraction (a crime usually not punishable by jail time), you should not have any immigration problems, unless the infraction involves theft or drugs, or the authorities determine that you are undocumented or that your visa has expired. Note that in some states, possession of a small amount of marijuana is merely an infraction, yet because this is a drug crime, it could have an effect on your immigration status.

The immigration consequences of criminal cases are different for minors than for adults. A non-U.S. citizen who is found delinquent (guilty) in juvenile court normally won't suffer any immigration consequences. However, crimes involving drug trafficking have serious immigration consequences for young people who are not lawful permanent residents. Even being charged with drug trafficking, let alone being proven to have done it, can result in expulsion, denial of re-entry, etc. Also, don't simply assume that a prior conviction was considered a juvenile offense, just because you were under 18 at the time—the age at which you're considered an adult varies from jurisdiction to jurisdiction, and minors are sometimes prosecuted as adults for certain offenses (see Chapter 11, Rights of Minors, page 122).

When plea bargaining, be especially careful about "diversion." Diversion is a procedure in which you do community service and/or pay an administrative fee, after which the charges against you are dismissed—so you don't get a conviction on your record. *However, if you are not a U.S. citizen, diversion usually counts as a conviction!* Non-U.S. citizens must have a local immigration attorney check

whether it's safe to take diversion in their particular region.

Some other procedures equivalent to diversion are "deferred prosecution" and "dispositional continuance." These programs also usually count as convictions for immigration purposes, if a plea of guilty or no contest is entered at any time. The bottom line is that if you are not a U.S. citizen, you must make sure you understand the exact immigration consequences of any plea bargain you accept. Do not trust a criminal defense lawyer's advice that a diversion program is safe, unless he has checked with an immigration lawyer—particularly if the diversion involves pleading guilty or no contest.

13

GETTING OUT OF JAIL WHILE YOUR CASE IS PENDING

The procedures for getting out of jail while your case is pending vary from state to state and from county to county. The vocabulary is pretty variable, too. However, the following options commonly available:

a) The officers at the police station or jail may release you, on a *promise to appear* (sometimes called a citation, summons or ticket).

b) If you're not allowed a promise to appear, you may be able to get out of jail by posting *bail*.

c) If you can't afford the initial bail amount, you can wait until you're taken to court, where you can ask the judge to lower your bail or release you on your *own recognizance*.

Promise to Appear: The best type of release from custody is when you simply sign a promise to come to court, without having to put up any money. It's usually a form that looks like a traffic ticket, offered by the law enforcement agency that arrested you. See samples, pages 31 and 32. You can be released on a promise to appear at various stages: at the scene of the arrest, at the police station, or at the jail. Generally speaking, officers aren't permitted to release you on promise to appear if you're charged with a felony or acts or violence, or if you have a warrant or an immigration hold.

Bail: Bail is money that you (or people acting on your behalf) pay to the court, to be forfeited if you don't appear at scheduled hearings. In most places, there's a list of standard bail amounts for misdemeanors and lesser felonies. So, if you can pay the pre-set bail for whatever you're charged with, you get out of custody right away, without waiting to go before a judge. Most jails accept bail 24 hours a day. The jail may require that bail be paid with cash, cashier's checks or money orders, but some jails take credit cards (call first and ask). When the case is over, the bail money is returned. However, in some circumstances, the judge can apply the bail money to fines or restitution (especially if the defendant used his own money for the bail). Check with a local lawyer or bail bondsman to make sure you know how bail is handled in your jurisdiction.

Own Recognizance: Release on your own recognizance is the same as a promise to appear, but it's granted by a judge rather than by the police. The judge accepts your word that you'll come to court, without demanding bail. There is considerable variation in names for this procedure: own recognizance (OR), release on your own recognizance (ROR), personal recognizance (PR), etc.

Generally, release on bail or on your own recognizance involves a degree of court supervision. The conditions may include: restricted travel, stay-away orders, and periodic reporting to a supervising officer.

In nearly all jurisdictions, minors are not entitled to bail. If a minor is released while a case is pending, it will normally be on his own recognizance under court supervision.

PREPARING FOR A BAIL HEARING

A bail hearing is any court appearance at which you ask the judge to release you from custody pending the outcome of your case. It's still called a bail hearing, even though you may be asking for release on your own recognizance, rather than bail. Often, a bail hearing is just part of a longer hearing involving other procedures, such as entering a plea or arguing a motion. You can have multiple bail hearings, and persistence pays off: sometimes a judge finally decides to let you out of jail at your fourth or fifth bail hearing. It helps, of course, to present new evidence or arguments each time you request release.

To be released, you'll have to persuade the judge that:

(1) you're not a danger to the community; and

(2) you're not a flight risk.

Certain factors make it tougher—and sometimes impossible—to get out of jail. The judge is less likely to order your release if you:

- have an outstanding warrant

- got arrested again while you were already out on a promise to appear, bail, or OR

- are on probation or parole

- have failed to appear for court dates in the past

- have immigration problems

- were arrested for a violent crime

- were arrested with weapons in your possession

On the bright side, there are easy ways to improve your chances at a bail hearing. The main task is to supply your lawyer with proof that you're not a flight risk. Your lawyer will be arguing to the judge that you have long-term ties to the community, and therefore you wouldn't just leave and never come back. So you (and the family and friends who are helping you) should look for **witnesses** and **documents** that might assist your lawyer in convincing the judge that you won't skip town.

Communicating at a Bail Hearing

Generally, your lawyer will do the talking. If you try to speak to the judge without being directed to do so by your lawyer, the judge will be annoyed. So, it's important that you tell your lawyer about your ties to the community and any negative factors *before* your case is called.

Although you won't be speaking, the judge will look carefully at you, trying to tell whether you're reliable. Therefore, your facial expression and body language count for a great deal. Of course, if you were arrested the day before, you'll probably be feeling upset, sleep-deprived, and ill. But you'll only be in court for five minutes, so for that window of time, you've got to pull yourself together and look dependable and alert. Try to tidy yourself, before entering the courtroom. Don't look angry, even if you were wrongfully arrested. Don't let your gaze wander, but keep your attention focused on the judge. Don't cross your arms over your chest (which looks challenging), but stand up straight and behave with respectful dignity.[1]

Remember, you're not allowed to fight your case at the bail hearing. Your lawyer may point out weaknesses in the prosecution's claims, in arguing that bail should be reduced, but the judge won't listen to the story of what really happened. The only issue being decided is whether to let you out of jail; that is, what it will take to make sure you come to court.

Witnesses for a Bail Hearing:

- relatives, especially parents and children
- employers or business partners
- landlord
- religious professionals (minister, priest, monk, nun, rabbi, imam)
- teachers or professors
- counselors

The witnesses (and even the people who are simply there to show support) should be conservatively dressed, not wearing gang colors or t-shirts with slogans on them. The people who speak or write letters on your behalf must be able to say that they know you well, and that you're a reliable person who will surely come to court whenever you're supposed to. It does more harm than good if a character witness says hesitantly, "Well, I kind of know him, and I think he'd probably come to court…"

Being positive and assertive is particularly important for families who are trying to keep custody of a minor who's been picked up for criminal activity.[2] Before a detention hearing in juvenile court, family members should talk with the minor's lawyer about how to convince the judge to let their kid come back home. In court, the family should firmly promise to help the young person follow whatever rules and programs the judge sets up. If the family members don't speak with confidence, the judge may feel that they don't have enough commitment or enough parenting skills to provide adequate structure for the minor.[3]

Documents for a Bail Hearing:

- deed or lease, rent receipts, utility bills, phone bills (both current bills and very old ones, to show the span of time you've been at this residence)
- employment contract, pay stubs, records of volunteer work (both current and old records)
- school i.d., school records
- proof of membership in community organizations or churches
- character reference letters from: employers, landlords, religious professionals, teachers and counselors (saying only that you're a reliable person who will surely come to court, *not* discussing the case itself)
- list of character references with phone numbers
- letters on doctor's stationery about any medical conditions or appointments that necessitate your release (saying, for example, that you're scheduled to have surgery next week)

It's good to provide the original of each document (for the judge), plus three copies (for the prosecutor, the defense attorney, and yourself). Obviously, it can be very difficult for friends and family to run around trying to

---

1. This is a good opportunity to see whether you have any latent telepathic skills that might manifest during an emergency. Transmit loudly and clearly: "I am not a flight risk, I am a pillar of the community," or thoughts to that effect.

2. In most jurisdictions, there's no bail for juveniles. So the family must concentrate on persuading the judge that *they* will make sure the minor comes to court, since they can't just "ransom" him.

3. If family members feel they must yell at their kid, they should do it someplace other than the courtroom or the hallway of the courthouse.

assemble these materials while you're sitting in jail. It makes a lot of sense to keep such papers organized in a safe but accessible place, so that you can tell people where to look.

Official Reports for Determining Release on Your Own Recognizance

In some places, there's an agency that creates reports for the court concerning the defendant's community ties, to help the judge decide whether or not to release him on OR. The people preparing these reports may be part of the probation department, part of pretrial services, or from an outside organization. Generally, they meet with prisoners who've just been arrested, but haven't yet been to court, and ask questions about address, length of residence, employment, etc. They'll want phone numbers, so they can call and confirm the information you provide. Naturally, cooperating with such a report is to your advantage. It's helpful, if you've been able to call your friends and family, to have them locate the phone numbers you'll want to give this interviewer. It's also important to let people know that they should go ahead and speak to whomever calls concerning the report. The one danger here is that you, or one of your contacts, might be talking to a police detective or other law enforcement agent, by mistake. So make sure that the person who's asking you questions is just preparing an OR report. The individual should have appropriate identification, and should not be asking questions about anything other than community ties and character references. Unless you're absolutely sure you're talking to someone who's preparing an OR report, say the Magic Words: *I'm going to remain silent. I would like to see a lawyer.* The worst that can happen, if it turns out that the interviewer was legitimate and you didn't answer his questions, is that you'll have to get your friends and your lawyer to provide this sort of information to the court, instead of relying on the report. If you have a good support network, they can be more effective than any agency in assembling material to prove your community ties.

Last Minute Preparation for a Bail Hearing

If you're about to appear for a bail hearing and there's been no OR interview and no time to assemble witnesses or documents, at least ask your attorney to call your relatives, employer, landlord, school, etc. That way, your lawyer will be able to tell the judge that she's made these calls and verified your address and that you're employed, paying rent, attending classes, etc. There may only be a few moments in which to undertake this task, so work on getting the names and phone numbers ready to give your lawyer.

WORKING WITH A BAIL BONDSMAN

Bondsmen make a living by lending people money for bail.[4] Normally, defendants (or their friends or family) pay a bondsman 10% of the total bail for making this loan. This 10% is the bondsman's fee—it's not given back when the case is over.

For example, if your bail were $10,000, you'd pay $1,000 to the bondsman. Then the bondsman would give the court a "surety bond" for $10,000.[5] As long as you made all your court appearances, the surety bond would be dissolved at the end of the case. So the bondsman's profit would be the $1,000 you paid him at the outset. However, if you skipped town and weren't caught, the bondsman would have to pay the court $10,000.

So bondsmen won't agree to make bail for just anyone— they look at the very same factors, positive and negative, that judges consider in evaluating a defendant for bail. Also, bondsmen much prefer to have a co-signor to the bail contract. The co-signor is a relative or friend who promises to pay the entire amount of the bail (reimbursing the bondsman for the surety bond), if you go on permanent vacation. The bondsman is a surety to the court, and the co-signor is a surety to the bondsman.

Before calling a bondsman, have all your information ready (character references, phone numbers, credit card numbers, bank account numbers, etc.), so that you can make the phone call as efficient as possible. If you're calling from jail, you may have very limited time to use the phone, so you'll need to be well-organized (and this will also be a point in your favor with the bondsman).

---

4. Four states—Illinois, Kentucky, Oregon, and Wisconsin—do not have bail bondsmen. They still have bail, but their legislatures have prohibited the business of making bail bonds. Some of these states do allow the payment of 10% of the bail, rather than the whole amount, but it goes to the court, not to a bondsman.

5. Surety (shŏŏr´ə-tē), is derived from the same Latin root as the word "insurance." In this context, a surety is the person who promises to pay a loan, if the actual debtor fails to do so.

Bondsmen often require collateral, in addition to 10% of the total bail. The collateral is returned to whomever-whoever provided it, once the case is concluded and the surety bond is dissolved. Collateral can be a piece of land, a house, a business, stocks or bonds, a life insurance policy, a vehicle, or even jewelry. Some bondsmen will only accept liens[6] on land or houses. It's important to realize that collateral is forfeit if the defendant skips town. For example, if someone's house is put up as collateral and the defendant disappears, the house can be seized.[7]

Collateral can also be cash, which is always acceptable. Cash collateral is money paid to the bondsman, beyond his fee. The bondsman returns the cash collateral, once the case is over (unlike the fee, usually 10% of the total bail, which the bondsman keeps).

If defendants refuse to come to court or if they run away, they can be arrested and kept in custody by the bondsmen and their "recovery agents" (bounty hunters), who then turn the defendants over to the authorities.

Note that most bondsmen charge an additional fee (another 10% of the total bail) each year, because they have to renew the surety bond. So if the case drags on for more than 12 months, and many do, you might have to pay the bondsman more money. Check with your lawyer about alternatives, such as getting the bail reduced or "exonerated" (terminated), or posting collateral with the court. Start dealing with this at least a month before the year is up, so that you won't be rushed.

Bondsmen don't always charge 10% of the bail as their fee. Sometimes they can charge a lower rate, such as 8%, if the bail is very large, or the defendant has a private attorney, or is a union member, etc. The range within which bondsmen can set their fees is governed by state law. Definitely check with your lawyer if the bondsman is quoting you a rate that's over 10%.

Bondsmen are licensed by the state in which they operate. If the bondsman's license number isn't on his business card or paperwork, ask to see the license before doing business (this is understood as common sense, not rudeness). Make sure to read and keep copies of all the paperwork you do with the bondsman, especially the documents you sign.

When should you seek the services of a bondsman? The answer depends on several factors:

- Can your friends and family can make bail themselves, instead of going through a bondsman? It's possible to save lots of money this way, since the bondsman's 10% fee is non-refundable—even if the charges are dismissed as soon as the defendant gets to court.[8]

- Can a lawyer can get the bail lowered? Most private criminal defense lawyers will talk to you for free for a little while, as both parties need to have some discussion to decide whether or not to work together. One of the important issues to bring up is whether the lawyer thinks the judge will reduce the bail. Say the initial bail was $100,000, but at the bail hearing, the lawyer gets the judge to lower it to $20,000. By waiting for the hearing, you'd have saved a lot of money. If you were making the bail yourself, you'd have kept $80,000 from being tied up. And if you were going through a bondsman, you'd have saved $8,000 (because you'd pay the bondsman $2,000 instead of $10,000).

- Can you stand to stay in jail for a while? Generally, to get the bail lowered, the defendant will have to remain in jail for a day, or perhaps several days, until the bail hearing. Some people feel they can stick it out, while others need to be bailed out immediately.[9] Explain your priorities to your friends and family, so they don't just assume what you'd want. If their resources are really limited, make sure to tell them whether to spend money on a bondsman, a lawyer, or neither.

---

6. A "lien" is the right to take possession of a particular item of property, if a debt isn't paid. For example, if a house is being used as collateral for a bail bond, the bondsman will "take a lien on the house."

7. People who put up bail or collateral really can lose everything when a defendant skips town. Too many grandmothers have ended up broke and homeless this way.

8. Watch out, however, if you use a credit card to pay the bail. The interest rates on credit cards can be very high, so it's important to pay the balance or get it transferred to a card with a low interest rate, if the case isn't going to be resolved right away.

9. A little time in jail can be a golden opportunity to gather material for the best-selling book you plan to write.

14

REPORTING POLICE MISCONDUCT

A great deal of police misconduct occurs, but goes unreported.[1] This is a shame for several reasons:

- Reporting police misconduct is the first step in stopping it.
- Reporting police misconduct may help a victim win a lawsuit against the officers who injured him.
- Reporting police misconduct may help show that a defendant in a criminal case was coerced by officers to confess or consent to a search.

One reason many people don't report police misconduct they've seen or experienced, is that they're not sure how to go about it. The following material will help you provide clear and powerful testimony, if you're in a position to report police misconduct.

There are three tricks to being a good eyewitness:

1. **Learn in advance what categories of information will be relevant in court, so you can catch the right details. That's why you should familiarize yourself with the Police Misconduct Report form now (page 140).**

2. **Describe what's happening in words, while you're witnessing it. By mentally giving a running commentary on the action, you make much stronger memories.**

3. **Write down everything that happened. Don't wait—do it immediately after the incident. If at all possible, make notes while you're still at the scene, especially about names and numbers.**

Experiments have shown that our minds don't normally retain very many details of our experiences.[2] There's also a myth in our society that when you see a shocking event, it's branded into your memory and under the right circumstances (such as hypnosis) you'll be able to play it back, just like a videotape. That's rarely true. The reality is that if you're very angry or afraid, your mind stores *fewer* of the details that you're experiencing, because your attention is divided. For example, it's not unusual for rape victims to find themselves unable to remember even their assailant's race or hair color. So, if you're experiencing or watching police violence or threats (which is naturally upsetting), you'll have to concentrate carefully to see and remember the details. You'll do a much better job if you say in your mind exactly what's going on while you're watching, the same as a sports announcer. It might sound like this:

> Now there's five, six, no *seven* cops, all piling on him! They've got him pinned to the ground. They're handcuffing him. Okay, they've rolled him over on his back…and what are they doing? Oh, man, they're spraying mace or something right in his face! He's coughing and gagging. The cops keep on spraying him, over and over. He's trying to twist away, but they're all holding him down. Damn, they've used up that whole thing of spray on him— nothing more is coming out! He's not breathing too good either, he's straining for air, with his mouth wide open and his head thrown back… Whoa, that big cop just kicked him in the ribs!

If you have a cell phone with you, call a voice mail or a message machine and record your play-by-play description. And then make a copy of your message afterward, before it gets erased. Your "live coverage" could be very powerful evidence, both in court and in the media.[3]

POLICE MISCONDUCT REPORT

The incident report form on the following pages was created by several lawyers,[4] to help witnesses to and victims of police misconduct record what they experienced. Naturally, no one will be able to answer every single question on this form. The point is just to write down all the information you do have, before it fades away. And memories evaporate quickly. The best time to fill out the police misconduct report is within a few hours of the incident. Even by the next day, you'll find it much harder to remember critical details. To do a good job, you need to be familiar with the form *before* you witness the incident. Otherwise, when it comes time to fill it out, you'll be kicking yourself because you missed lots of information that you could've collected, if only you'd known it was important. So read through the police mis-

---

1. For more information on police misconduct and what can be done about it, see Appendix B: Suggested Reference Material on Police Misconduct, page 182.

2. To learn more about providing accurate eyewitness testimony, see Elizabeth F. Loftus, *Eyewitness Testimony* (Cambridge, MA: Harvard University Press, 1996). It's important to know which details require greater concentration, such as: remembering the features of someone of a different race, noticing other facts when someone's brandishing a weapon, and perceiving details during a stressful or violent incident.

3. Even if you do record the event using your cell phone, you must also fill out the police misconduct report right away. The questions in the report will help you remember material that you didn't happen to talk about while you were making your recording. The written report and the spoken recording will each make the other stronger.

4. The lawyers who designed this police misconduct report form are: Katya Komisaruk, Osha Neumann, and Bill Simpich.

conduct report form now. Better yet, practice actually filling out the form, using the material from the story *Protect and Serve* (page 150) or your own experiences. Afterward, look at the sample report (page 157) describing the events in *Protect and Serve.* If you take the time to work with the police misconduct report in advance, you'll get the outline of it in your head, so that when you're at an incident, you'll know just what information to seek out. (You can make photocopies of the form that's in the book, or you can download a copy from the Just Cause Law Collective website: http://www.lawcollective.org/.)

POLICE MISCONDUCT REPORT

submitted to attorney _____ in anticipation of litigation

- **If you don't know the answers** to some of the following questions, **leave the box blank**. It's okay if you didn't see every single thing.

- **Don't guess**! Even one false answer can ruin your whole report, because people assume that if one answer is wrong, then none of your answers are trustworthy.

- If a question concerns **locations or distance, go back to the scene and check**.

ABOUT YOU	
Today's date:	
Name:	Email:
Address:	
Phone numbers:	

ABOUT THE INCIDENT	
Date of incident:	
Time incident began:	Time incident ended:
Exact location of incident:	

ABOUT MEDIA WITNESSES
If there were reporters, photographers or videographers present, give names, descriptions, phone numbers, emails, and media organization.

ABOUT OTHER WITNESSES
Description, name, address, email and phone numbers:

If the incident involved more than one police officer or victim, use additional copies of this page. For example, if there were two officers, you would need one extra copy of this page. If there are more than one victim or officer, and you don't know their names, call them victim-1, victim-2, victim-3, or officer-1, officer-2, officer-3, etc.

ABOUT THE VICTIM	
Name:	Email:
Address:	
Phone numbers:	
Gender:	Age:
Race:	Complexion:
Height:	Weight:
Hair (color, type, style):	Facial hair:
Glasses:	Voice (high/low, accent):
Marks, scars, tattoos:	Disabilities:
Clothing:	

ABOUT THE OFFICER	
Name:	
Organization:	
Badge number:	Rank:
Gender:	Age:
Race:	Complexion:
Height:	Weight:
Hair (color, type, style):	Facial hair:
Glasses:	Voice (high/low, accent):
Clothing/uniform, weapons:	
Vehicle (make, markings, license):	

If the incident involved more than one police officer or victim, use additional copies of this page. For example, if there were two officers, you would need one extra copy of this page. If there are more than one victim or officer, and you don't know their names, call them victim-1, victim-2, victim-3, or officer-1, officer-2, officer-3, etc.

ABOUT THE VICTIM	
Name:	Email:
Address:	
Phone numbers:	
Gender:	Age:
Race:	Complexion:
Height:	Weight:
Hair (color, type, style):	Facial hair:
Glasses:	Voice (high/low, accent):
Marks, scars, tattoos:	Disabilities:
Clothing:	

ABOUT THE OFFICER	
Name:	
Organization:	
Badge number:	Rank:
Gender:	Age:
Race:	Complexion:
Height:	Weight:
Hair (color, type, style):	Facial hair:
Glasses:	Voice (high/low, accent):
Clothing/uniform, weapons:	
Vehicle (make, markings, license):	

COMMANDING OFFICER	
Name:	
Organization:	
Badge number:	Rank:

ABOUT WHAT LED UP TO THE INCIDENT

What happened leading up to the incident? What was going on when police arrived? What did the victim do? What did the officer do? What did they say?

ABOUT OFFICIAL ORDERS

Were orders given (to disperse, to lie down, etc.)? Who issued the order and what did they say? Did you or others have trouble hearing the order? If so, why?

ABOUT WHAT HAPPENED DURING THE INCIDENT

What did the officer and victim say during and after the incident? Did you hear the officer use swear words or hate speech (racist, sexist or anti-gay words)? Did the officer say anything that was rude, unfair or untrue? What tones of voice did people use?

Did the officer ask permission to search any person or place (bag, car, home)? How did the victim respond? What did the officer do then?

Did you see violence? Who was involved? What kind of violence was used (slap, punch, kick, arm-twisting, chokehold, pepper spray, nightstick, gunshot)? How many times was the victim struck? What part of the body was targeted? What position was the victim in (standing, bent over, kneeling or lying down)? Was the victim handcuffed or being held down?

(continue on next page)

ABOUT WHAT HAPPENED DURING THE INCIDENT

(continue from previous page)

ABOUT PROPERTY

Was anyone's property damaged or taken away? When and how?

ABOUT WRONGFUL SEARCHES OR ARRESTS

Did the officer search the wrong person or place (car, home)? Was the wrong person arrested? Was there a warrant? What person or place was specified in the warrant?

ABOUT INJURIES TO VICTIM

What were the number and location of the victim's injuries (scrapes, bruises, cuts, sprains, broken bones, bullet wounds)? If victim died, where and when did it happen?

Describe any ambulance or medical staff which came (name, license plate, i.d. number):

Name, address and phone numbers of anyone with photographs or videotape of victim's injuries (during or after the incident):

Go back to the scene of the incident and draw a diagram of the area. Show where you were during the incident. Show where the victim and officer were. Put in other landmarks like: signs, parked cars, fences, benches, etc. Use arrows to show where people moved.

WHAT TO DO WITH THE POLICE MISCONDUCT REPORT

Always keep the original copy of a police misconduct report you've filled out. Make photocopies of your report for other people as needed. Never give away your only copy.

Deliver your information to the victim or the victim's attorney within a week. That way, if the victim has been charged with a crime, his criminal defense attorney will have a better chance of heading off the case. And if the victim wants to sue the police, his civil rights lawyer won't miss the deadlines—some as short as two weeks—for the first steps in a lawsuit ("giving notice of claim").

How you use the police misconduct report depends on whether you're a victim or a witness, and on whether anyone expects to go to court.

1. **You're the victim. Choose (a) or (b) below.**

   (a) You've been charged with a crime and/or you're thinking of suing the police.

   > You must be sure to give the report only to your own lawyer(s). If you even show the police misconduct report to other people, it will no longer be protected by the attorney/client privilege—and that would be very disadvantageous in a legal battle (see Maintaining Confidentiality, page 174).

   (b) You're absolutely certain that you're not going to be charged with a crime and you're not going to sue the police.

   > Submit a complaint to the local police review organization. This may be a private community organization, it may be part of the city or county government, or it may be part of the police department. Normally, such an organization will have its own report form, usually much shorter than the police misconduct report. Attach a copy of the police misconduct report to the organization's form, so that you provide as much detail as possible.

   > (Although police review agencies rarely discipline police officers, your complaint may be helpful to another victim in the future. That victim's lawyer will seek out past complaints, to show that the officer has a history of abusive behavior.)

2. **You're a witness. Choose (a) or (b) below.**

   (a) The victim has been charged with a crime and/or is thinking of suing the police.

   > Give copies of the police misconduct report to the victim and the victim's lawyer(s).

   (b) The victim is definitely not going to be charged with a crime and is not going to sue the police.

   > Submit a complaint to the victim and to the police review organization, see 1(b). You don't have to be a victim to submit a complaint.

How to find the victim:

If you don't know the victim, try asking people in the area where the incident occurred (neighbors, workers, students). Be persistent. As a last resort, leave notices where the incident happened (on telephone poles, lampposts, fences, etc.), explaining that you witnessed police misconduct and are willing to talk to the victim. Give clear instructions on how to contact you. If you leave notices, the police may contact you, too, although you're certainly not required to speak with them.

How to find the criminal defense lawyer who is representing the victim:

If the victim has been charged with a crime, he should have a lawyer, either a private attorney or the public defender. First, you've got to get the victim's name. Once you have that, call the public defender's office and/or the office of court records,[5] and ask: "Has a case been filed against _____?" (Remember to refer to the victim of police misconduct as the "defendant," because you're asking about someone who's been charged with a crime.) If a case has been filed, ask for the name of the defendant's lawyer. (Make sure you're getting the name of the defense attorney, not the prosecutor.) Be polite but persistent. Sometimes it takes a few days for the charges to be filed and sometimes whoever answers the phone may not be able or willing to help. So be prepared to call back several times, or go to the courthouse or the public defender's office in person. (If the victim was arrested by federal officers or on federal property, make sure you call the clerk of the U.S. District Court or the Office of the Federal Defender.)

How to find a police misconduct lawyer:

You want a lawyer who does mostly police misconduct cases, not one who does a little of everything, or who handles some other area of law, like divorces or immigration. You can find a police misconduct lawyer by calling the local offices of the National Lawyers Guild (NLG), the National Association for the Advancement of Colored People (NAACP), the American Civil Liberties Union (ACLU), or the local bar association. Don't give up just because the first few lawyers say they can't help. If more than one lawyer is willing to take the case, interview them all to see which seems best. Usually, police misconduct cases are taken on contingency. This means that the victim doesn't pay her lawyer up front; instead, the victim's lawyer gets paid only if she wins the case—that's why police misconduct lawyers are very selective about which cases they'll accept. Your carefully written report may help convince a good lawyer to take the case in the first place, as well as being useful later on.[6]

Note: If there is a court case, you must check with the victim's lawyer before talking to reporters. Obviously, publicity can be extremely helpful to someone who's been victimized by the police, but you should work with the victim's attorney to determine the best way to go about this. You need to find the right journalists to talk to, choose exactly what to say, and decide just when to break the story. The staff of local chapters of the NLG, NAACP or ACLU often has considerable experience in arranging publicity for political cases. You may want to ask them to work with the victim's lawyer on fine-tuning the media strategy, writing press releases, etc.

---

5. The office in which court records are kept goes by various names, such as: the clerk's office, the clerk of the court, the criminal records division, the records department, etc. Be patient and expect to make several phone calls before you hit the right office. Sometimes there's one office for civil cases and another for criminal cases. Usually, the office has a counter or window, and if you go there in person, you can speak directly to a clerk.

6. When you're trying to get a lawyer to take a case on contingency, dress conservatively and be extremely organized. The lawyer will be checking you out, wondering whether you'd be helpful in preparing the case and believable in court. If you don't make a good impression at the first meeting, you may not get another chance.

PROTECT AND SERVE

Watch the video version of this story, to practice your witnessing skills in real-time! It's on the Just Cause Law Collective website: http://www.lawcollective.org/.

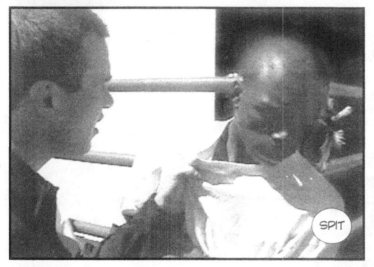

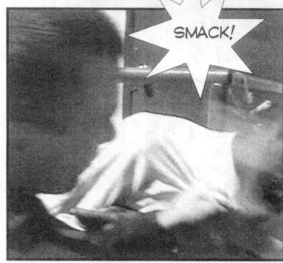

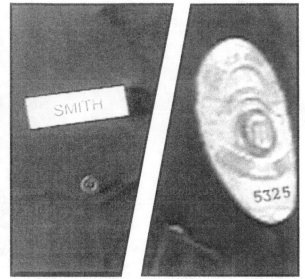

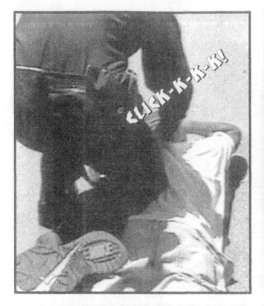

RUN AFTER THE MAN ON THE STEPS AND THE WOMAN ACROSS THE STREET AND GET THEIR CONTACT INFO. OTHERWISE YOU MAY NEVER BE ABLE TO FIND THEM. THEY MAY HAVE THEIR WEAKNESSES, BUT THEY SHOULD BE ABLE TO BACK YOU UP IN COURT. THREE WITNESSES ARE A LOT BETTER THAN ONE WHEN YOU'RE TESTIFYING AGAINST THE POLICE.

SO, THE OFFICERS ARE CLAIMING THAT ANTHONY AND CECILIA ATTACKED THEM! THESE KIDS MAY BE CONVICTED UNLESS YOU CAN EXPLAIN TO THE JUDGE WHAT REALLY HAPPENED. WILL YOUR TESTIMONY BE CONVINCING? TRY FILLING OUT THE POLICE MISCONDUCT REPORT TO SEE HOW MANY DETAILS YOU OBSERVED.

QUESTIONS AND ANSWERS ABOUT *PROTECT AND SERVE*

Why is it important to notice what was said and done *before* the police began threatening or hurting the victims?

Because you need to show who was at fault. The police may lie and claim that they were just responding to the *suspect's* being violent or running away.

Were Anthony and Cecilia responsible for starting the incident because they said something disrespectful about the police officers?

No. The right to freedom of speech means that anyone is entitled to criticize the police. It's not illegal to make rude remarks to a law enforcement officer.[7] And in this case, Anthony and Cecilia weren't even talking to the police, they were having a private conversation.

What about the other witnesses to this incident? Would they be helpful?

There were two other witnesses: a young man and a woman. The man looked like he might be afraid to get involved, and might have been drunk at the time (since he's holding a bag with a bottle). The woman seemed to be concerned about what was happening, because Officer Smith tried to reassure her by saying, "We've got everything under control here, ma'am! Nothing to worry about!" However, she may have been too far away to see and hear properly. Nonetheless, it's absolutely critical to talk to *both* witnesses and get their names and a way to contact them in the future. (If you don't make contact with them at the time of the incident, it may be impossible to find them later.) In a police misconduct case, the more witnesses, the better. If the officers lie about what happened, and it's your word against theirs, you really need other eyewitnesses to back up your testimony. Even when the other witnesses only saw or heard a small part of what happened, if they can support what you're saying, that will help.

If you're witnessing a police misconduct incident in real life, how close can you stand? Should you talk to the police or to the victim?

There's no law about how close you can be to the police—you've just got to use common sense. Get as near as possible, so you can see and hear details, without being in the officers' way. Remember that you *do* have the right to watch what the officers are doing—

observing the police is not "obstruction of justice" or "interfering with an officer." You also have a right to talk to the police or the suspect. But if the police say they don't want to talk to you, don't nag them. Don't come up behind a police officer. Don't touch an officer or his equipment or his vehicle. And avoid quick or sneaky-looking movements.

What about taking photos or videos of police misconduct, like the person who videotaped Rodney King being beaten?

If someone can hurry and get a camera, that would be great. But if you're the only witness, it's better to stay, using your eyes and writing notes—if you went away, you might miss something important. Again, you have to use your own judgment. If you have a cell phone, be sure to call a voice mail or phone machine and record a detailed, blow-by-blow description of what's happening.

Aren't you taking a chance, if you report police misconduct like this, that the police will come and harass you?

Yes, that is a chance that you're taking. You could try to report it anonymously, but lawyers, police review organizations, and the media are not likely to pay attention unless the person making the report is willing to testify. If you do want to report police misconduct, there are two things that will make you safer. First, make sure that lots of people know that you've made the report—that way, it will be clearer if the police do go after you, that they're just trying to get even. Second, get other witnesses to make reports, too, because there's safety in numbers. Only you can decide if it's a good idea for you to report police misconduct, given the circumstances in which you live. But remember, for things to get better, people have to be willing to speak out. As a wise man once said, "If I am not for myself, who will be for me? If I am only for myself, what am I? And if not now, when?"[8]

Were the search and the arrest unlawful, since the officers didn't think Anthony and Cecilia had committed a crime?

Yes, the search and the arrest were unlawful. The officers didn't even have reasonable suspicion (the amount of proof necessary to detain a suspect), let alone probable cause (the amount of proof necessary to search or arrest a suspect). The officers didn't think Anthony and Cecilia had committed a crime, but just

---

7. It would be illegal, however, to distract an officer who's in middle of arresting someone or carrying out some other job-related activity.

8. Hillel *Ethics of the Fathers* 1:14 (c. 30 B.C.E.).

wanted to check on them out of curiosity. Remember that Officer Jones says, "Let's see what these kids are up to." This statement is very significant, because it helps show that the police weren't justified even in detaining Anthony and Cecilia. This is a good example of why it's important to notice what's said *before* things get ugly.

What about when Anthony spat or when Cecilia ran away? Were those actions illegal?

Anthony's spitting may well have been illegal, since in many areas there are laws against spitting on the sidewalk. Cecilia wasn't breaking the law by running away, since the police didn't have a legal reason for detaining her. (If the police actually had a valid reason for detaining her, then running away would have been illegal.) Legal or not, spitting and running were provocative in this situation. However, even if Anthony and Cecilia had committed serious crimes, the police weren't justified in hurting them as they did, or in using hate speech.

Did the police use excessive force in dealing with Anthony and Cecilia?

Yes. The police are only allowed to use force that's in proportion to the force used by the suspect, and only in order to restrain the suspect (or defend themselves) during a lawful detention or arrest. If this had been a lawful detention, Officer Jones could have dealt with Anthony by turning him around and handcuffing him, but Jones shouldn't have slapped Anthony. Nor should Jones have jabbed him with a nightstick just for calling out to Cecilia. And if Cecilia had run away from a lawful detention, it would have been reasonable for Officer Smith to grab her and handcuff her. But he wouldn't be entitled to use a chokehold on her, or whack her on the back of the head while he was handcuffing her.

Was Officer Jones's demand to search Anthony's bag legal?

No. The police officers didn't have an adequate reason to suspect Anthony and Cecilia in the first place, therefore the officers weren't entitled to search their bags. So Anthony was right in refusing to let the police look in his bag—but he might have expressed it in a less challenging way. It's an advantage to say it formally, such as: *"I don't consent* to your searching my bag." That signals to police and lawyers that you know your rights.

Was Anthony guilty of resisting arrest?

No, Anthony was entitled to object verbally, and he didn't resist physically. It was legal and sensible for Anthony to exercise his civil rights by refusing to answer questions and refusing consent to search his bag.

When the police used the words, "nigger," "faggot," "bitch," and "fuckin' beaner," was that misconduct?

Yes. Using this type of language is always against police regulations. And such words would be important evidence that the police were committing an act of racial discrimination and/or a "hate crime."

Privileged and confidential

POLICE MISCONDUCT REPORT

submitted to attorney ___Clara Darrow___ in anticipation of litigation

---

- **If you don't know the answers** to some of the following questions, **leave the box blank**. It's okay if you didn't see every single thing.

- **Don't guess!** Even one false answer can ruin your whole report, because people assume that if one answer is wrong, then none of your answers are trustworthy.

- If a question concerns **locations or distance**, go back to the scene and check.

ABOUT YOU

Today's date: 4/1/03

Name: Chris Smith   Email: chris@smith.com

Address: 1983 42nd St., Metropolis WD 20500

Phone numbers: (202) 479-3030

ABOUT THE INCIDENT

Date of incident: 4/1/03

Time incident began: 1:50 pm.   Time incident ended: 2:10 pm.

Exact location of incident: In front of Room 12B, Metropolis High School, 1400 Rivera St., Metropolis WD

ABOUT MEDIA WITNESSES

If there were reporters, photographers or videographers present, give names, descriptions, phone numbers, emails, and media organization.

none present

ABOUT OTHER WITNESSES

Description, name, address, email and phone numbers:

Jason Pedlar (homeless person) male, white, mid-twenties, 6', 150 lbs., brown curly collar-length hair, no glasses, light mustache. Contact through Father Bill, St. Joseph the Worker Church, 1640 Addison St., Metropolis WD 20310, (202) 224-7292.

Kate Fairview (teacher at MHS) female, white, mid-thirties, 5'3", 120 lbs., black shoulder-length hair, no glasses. Contact through Metropolis High School, 1400 Rivera St., Metropolis WD 20330, (202) 224-7363 (main office).

If the incident involved more than one police officer or victim, use additional copies of this page. For example, if there were two officers, you would need one extra copy of this page. If there are more than one victim or officer, and you don't know their names, call them victim-1, victim-2, victim-3, or officer-1, officer-2, officer-3, etc.

ABOUT THE VICTIM

Name: Anthony	Email:
Address:	
Phone numbers:	
Gender: male	Age: about 17
Race: African American	Complexion: dark
Height: 6'1"	Weight: 140
Hair (color, type, style): black, nappy, very short	Facial hair: none
Glasses: none	Voice (high/low, accent): medium voice, California accent
Marks, scars, tattoos: none visible	Disabilities: none visible
Clothing: white t-shirt, baggy faded blue jeans, sneakers, backpack	

ABOUT THE OFFICER

Name: Bob Jones	
Organization: Metropolis Police Department	
Badge number: 5382	Rank: patrol officer
Gender: male	Age: mid-twenties
Race: White	Complexion: medium
Height: 6'	Weight: 150
Hair (color, type, style): dark brown, straight, short	Facial hair: none
Glasses: none	Voice (high/low, accent): medium voice, ordinary accent
Clothing/uniform, weapons: dark blue uniform, gun, baton	
Vehicle (make, markings, license):	

2

Privileged and Confidential

If the incident involved more than one police officer or victim, use additional copies of this page. For example, if there were two officers, you would need one extra copy of this page. If there are more than one victim or officer, and you don't know their names, call them victim-1, victim-2, victim-3, or officer-1, officer-2, officer-3, etc.

ABOUT THE VICTIM	
Name: Cecilia	Email:
Address:	
Phone numbers:	
Gender: female	Age: about 17
Race: Latina	Complexion: medium
Height: 5'4"	Weight: 130
Hair (color, type, style): black, very curly, below shoulder length	Facial hair:
Glasses: none	Voice (high/low, accent): medium voice, slight Spanish accent
Marks, scars, tattoos: none visible	Disabilities: none visible
Clothing: white t-shirt, gray hooded sweatshirt tied at waist, faded blue jeans, sneakers, beaded necklace	

ABOUT THE OFFICER	
Name: Smith	
Organization: Metropolis Police Department	
Badge number: 5325	Rank: patrol officer
Gender: male	Age: mid-twenties
Race: White	Complexion: medium
Height: 6'3"	Weight: 160
Hair (color, type, style): blond, straight, short	Facial hair: none
Glasses: sunglasses in pocket	Voice (high/low, accent): medium voice, country accent
Clothing/uniform, weapons: dark blue uniform, gun, baton	
Vehicle (make, markings, license):	

3

COMMANDING OFFICER	
Name:	
Organization:	
Badge number:	Rank:

ABOUT WHAT LED UP TO THE INCIDENT

What happened leading up to the incident? What was going on when police arrived? What did the victim do? What did the officer do? What did they say?

Two teenagers, Anthony and Cecilia, were in front of Room 12B at Metropolis High School, talking to each other. Officers Smith and Jones were walking across the street toward them. On the way, Jones said to Smith, "Let's see what these kids are up to." Anthony and Cecilia were leaning with their backs against the stair railing, and the officers came and stood right in front of them, so the kids couldn't go anywhere. Smith asked, "What are you doing here? You got some i.d.?" Anthony answered, "You got eyes. You can see. We're just hanging out talking." And Cecilia said, "Why don't you leave us alone? We're not doing anything." Both officers looked annoyed at this. Then Jones said, "What's in the backpack? You got something in there?" And Anthony answered, "Man, I don't gotta show you nothing. This is bullshit!"

ABOUT OFFICIAL ORDERS

Were orders given (to disperse, to lie down, etc.)? Who issued the order and what did they say? Did you or others have trouble hearing the order? If so, why?

Jones told Anthony to "stay put" three times. Smith told Cecilia "Hold it!" and "Come back here!" Smith also told Cecilia to "shut up" twice.
It was easy to hear everything because there was no traffic at all, and no one was making any noise over in the schoolyard.

ABOUT WHAT HAPPENED DURING THE INCIDENT

What did the officer and victim say during and after the incident? Did you hear the officer use swear words or hate speech (racist, sexist or anti-gay words)? Did the officer say anything that was rude, unfair or untrue? What tones of voice did people use?

Did the officer ask permission to search any person or place (bag, car, home)? How did the victim respond? What did the officer do then?

Did you see violence? Who was involved? What kind of violence was used (slap, punch, kick, arm-twisting, chokehold, pepper spray, nightstick, gunshot)? How many times was the victim struck? What part of the body was targeted? What position was the victim in (standing, bent over, kneeling or lying down)? Was the victim handcuffed or being held down?

Jones asked to see what was in Anthony's backpack, and Anthony refused. Smith appeared really irritated, but Jones just grinned and asked, "You think you're pretty smart, don't ya nigger?" Anthony looked kind of shocked and said, "What did you say? Don't nobody say that shit to me! Jones took a step nearer to Anthony and ordered, "Stay put." And Anthony replied, "Man, I ain't stayin' nowhere. I don't got to do what you say, 'cause I wasn't doin' nothing wrong." Then Jones reached out with his left hand and grabbed a handful of Anthony's t-shirt, holding it in his fist under Anthony's chin. Jones was glaring at Anthony and bending close, so their faces were about 12" apart. Jones said, "When I say 'stay put,' I mean your little faggot ass stays right here with me!" Anthony was trying to lean away, but Jones had him pushed back against the railing. Jones said (right in Anthony's face), "You got a problem with me, nigger?" So Anthony, who hadn't said anything back, turned his head all the way to the left and spat on the ground. And Jones slapped him (once) with his right hand, backhanding Anthony hard across the face.

At this point, Cecilia, who was standing just to Anthony's right, tried to get away. She started to run across the street, and Smith ordered, "Hold it!" Cecilia kept on running and Smith chased her, yelling, "Come back here, you little bitch!" He caught her on the other side of the street, in front of the schoolyard's chain-link fence (where it meets a building, by the gas meters). He grabbed her and she didn't struggle at all, but Smith went ahead and used a chokehold on her, with his right arm across her throat. She made gagging noises, then appeared to pass out — her eyes were shut and she was hanging limply in Smith's arms. He laid her on the ground, on her face.

(continue on next page)

ABOUT WHAT HAPPENED DURING THE INCIDENT

(continue from previous page)

Anthony didn't even try to go anywhere — Jones was standing in front of him, holding his baton horizontally shoved up against Anthony's chest, so that Anthony was pinned against the railing. But Anthony was watching what Smith was doing to Cecilia across the street, and he yelled out, "Stop! You're hurting her!" Jones said, "I thought I told you to stay put!" And he took his baton and jabbed the end of it really hard and fast into Anthony's belly. Anthony groaned and doubled up, then sank to his knees. Jones pushed him so that he was lying face down, then knelt on his back and handcuffed him.

Meanwhile, Cecilia woke up while Smith was handcuffing her. Smith had his right knee in the small of her back, and she said, "Get off me!" Smith stayed where he was, cuffing her left hand and saying, "Shut up." As he pulled her right hand back, Cecilia begged, "Please get off! You're hurting me!" Smith finished cuffing her and snapped, "I said shut up, you fuckin' beaner!" Then, still kneeling on her, he smacked her once on the back of the head with his right hand. He pulled her to her feet, then walked her back to where Jones was cuffing Anthony, in front of Room 12B. As they were crossing the street, Cecilia asked, "How come you're doing this to us?" And Smith said, "Well, I reckon you'll have plenty of time at juvie to figure it out. You can start by considering what comes of having a big mouth and a bad attitude." Then the officers made both kids kneel on the sidewalk while they waited for a van to pick them up.

I could see everything really well because I was only 15'-20' away from all that was going on. It was a clear day and there were no trees or cars blocking my view. Jason Pedlar saw everything, too. He was sitting on some steps about 15' from the entrance to Room 12B. He was drinking from a bottle that was in a paper bag, but he seemed perfectly coherent when I talked to him. He wasn't confused or slurring his speech at all. Kate Fairview saw much of what happened, too. She was across the street from Room 12B, about 40' from Anthony and Jones, but only 15' from where Smith was choking Cecilia. After he'd cuffed Cecilia and taken her back across the street, Smith noticed Fairview watching him and called to her, "We've got everything under control here, ma'am! Nothing to worry about!"

6

ABOUT PROPERTY

Was anyone's property damaged or taken away? When and how?

The officers took Anthony's backpack, after they handcuffed him.

ABOUT WRONGFUL SEARCHES OR ARRESTS

Did the officer search the wrong person or place (car, home)? Was the wrong person arrested? Was there a warrant? What person or place was specified in the warrant?

The officers didn't say anything about an arrest warrant or a search warrant, and they didn't show any documents to Anthony or Cecilia. Jones kind of asked to see what was in Anthony's pack, but his tone of voice made it sound like an order, plus he and Smith were standing right in front of the kids so they couldn't leave.

ABOUT INJURIES TO VICTIM

What were the number and location of the victim's injuries (scrapes, bruises, cuts, sprains, broken bones, bullet wounds)? If victim died, where and when did it happen?

Anthony was slapped across the face once, and jabbed in the belly once with a baton. The second injury made him clutch his stomach and sink to the ground. Cecilia was choked and then smacked on the back of the head once. Cecilia appeared to be unconscious for a few minutes, after the choking. Her throat was reddened, too

Describe any ambulance or medical staff which came (name, license plate, i.d. number):

No ambulance or medical staff showed up. The officers didn't ask the kids if they needed any medical assistance.

Name, address and phone numbers of anyone with photographs or videotape of victim's injuries (during or after the incident):

Privileged and Confidential

Go back to the scene of the incident and draw a diagram of the area. Show where you were during the incident. Show where the victim and officer were. Put in other landmarks like: signs, parked cars, fences, benches, etc. Use arrows to show where people moved.

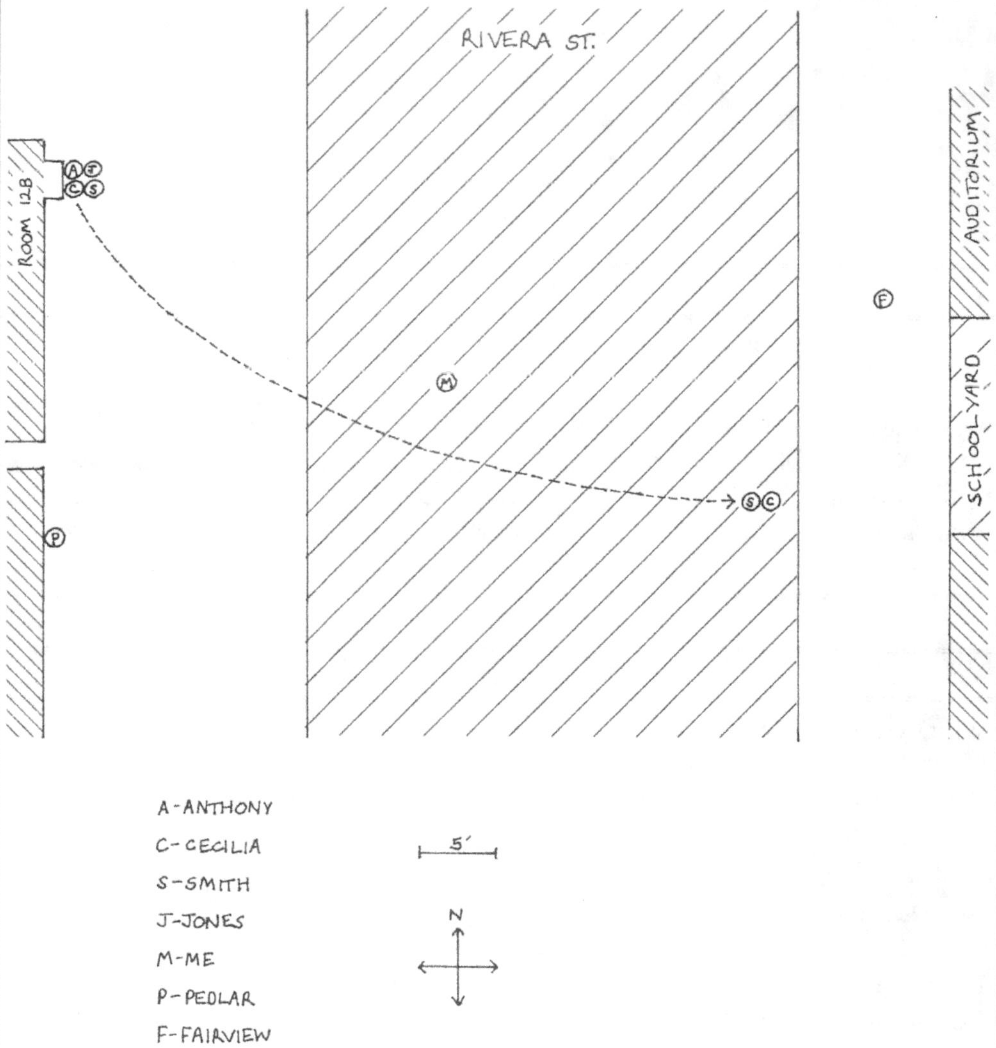

RIVERA ST.
ROOM 128
AUDITORIUM
SCHOOLYARD
A-ANTHONY
C-CECILIA
S-SMITH
J-JONES
M-ME
P-PEDLAR
F-FAIRVIEW
5′
N

15

WORKING EFFECTIVELY
WITH LAWYERS

SELECTING A LAWYER

If you're shopping for a lawyer, it's chancy to rely on advertisements from the yellow pages, billboards, or TV. Many good attorneys don't advertise at all, but just get clients by relying on word of mouth. So try getting referrals from:

- friends and acquaintances who've used particular attorneys and been pleased with their performance;

- other attorneys—most lawyers have a good sense of their local colleagues' reputations, at least in their own area of practice;

- bail bondsmen (though bondsmen may just be returning favors to attorneys who've referred clients to *them*).

Referrals from county bar associations aren't necessarily of much value. Many bar associations simply charge attorneys a fee for putting them on the association's referral list, and don't sort the members according to quality. So when you call the bar association, they may just be referring you to whichever attorney is next on the list as they rotate through all the names.

When an attorney says that she's a "state certified specialist" in criminal law, that's significant, because it means she's met extra requirements established by her state's bar association. Certification as a specialist usually involves passing an exam, taking additional continuing education classes, having practiced that area of law for least five years, and having done a substantial number of serious trials. States that certify lawyers as criminal law specialists include:

Arizona	New Jersey
California	New Mexico
Florida	North Carolina
Idaho	

The National Board of Trial Advocacy also certifies specialists in criminal law. Their website, from which you can obtain referrals, is: http://www.nbta.net/.

Don't be overly impressed by criminal defense attorneys who claim that they're better because they used to be prosecutors. Connections with the prosecutor's office don't necessarily produce better plea bargains—that has more to do with the experience, personality and negotiating skills of the particular attorney. And if you're going to trial, you may be better off with a former public defender, who will have had lots of practice actually defending cases, as opposed to prosecuting them.

Being a member of various professional organizations usually isn't significant—it depends on how many sets of membership dues the attorney is willing to pay. Neither is it very important which law school the lawyer attended—what counts is accomplishments while practicing law.

Nearly all criminal defense attorneys give free consultations. It makes sense to interview several, so that you have a choice. You might want to ask how many years the lawyer's been in practice and how much of that was spent doing criminal defense. It's also good to know how many trials the lawyer's done, and how many cases involving your charges.

If you're having trouble deciding between two lawyers, try asking whether they would be willing to work together, sharing the fee. Assuming they get along, both of them may prefer such an arrangement, because they can strategize together, and then each can focus on the parts of the case he does best. Besides, attorneys like to have a partner during trial, a process that always involves a great deal of work and stress.

When you interview an attorney, make sure you're clear on exactly how much money you'd be paying if you hired her. Criminal defense attorneys are normally paid a flat fee in advance. They don't take cases on contingency and rarely charge by the hour. Often, a criminal defense lawyer will charge half the fee if the case settles (through a plea bargain or dismissal), and require the second half of the fee only if the case goes to trial. Some attorneys break the fee into thirds in felony cases, when those fall naturally into three stages. Most criminal defense lawyers also expect the client to pay separately for "costs," such as travel, investigation, experts, etc. All this should be in the fee agreement (contract)—do not sign it until you understand every single part of it.

WORKING WITH A PUBLIC DEFENDER

As you remember, you have the right to an attorney and if you cannot afford one, the court will appoint one for you. This means that each jurisdiction has to make arrangements to provide such lawyers, usually by maintaining a public defender's office. There will also be a system for supplying additional lawyers when the public defender's office has too many cases or a conflict of interest. In this situation, the court will typically appoint an attorney from a panel of private lawyers or a designated law office. (These might be called "panel attorneys," "conflicts attorneys," "court-appointed attorneys," "alternate defenders," etc.)

To get the best possible service from a public defender, you need to understand the breed. First, there are easier and more profitable positions for law school graduates than working as a public defender. There's a myth that being a public defender is a kind of internship or mandatory service period—some people even imagine that you have to be a public defender first, in order to become a prosecutor. The truth is that getting a job in a public defender's office can be highly competitive in some areas of the country—many offices can take their pick of the top students from the best law schools, and there are sometimes several hundred applicants for a single position. Few public defenders ever switch sides and become prosecutors. People who become prosecutors are usually either law-and-order types, or beginning lawyers who just want to get lots of trial experience quickly. People who become public defenders normally take the job because they really want to help low-income people and keep them out of jail.

This isn't to say that there aren't public defenders who are incompetent, lazy, or mean. It's just that you're as likely to encounter bad private attorneys as bad public defenders. The real difference between public defenders and private attorneys is the number of clients they handle. Public defenders have huge caseloads, much larger than that of private criminal defense attorneys. Also, public defenders' offices have relatively limited budgets for hiring investigators and expert witnesses. So most public defenders can't give their clients as much personal attention as they'd like, or prepare every case for trial as well as they'd prefer.[1] You'll usually see the public defenders in court with heaps of file folders stacked on the defense table, each of which relates to a different client who must be taken care of that day.[2]

So your mission, if you're working with a public defender, is to make it clear that you're a client who can really be helped, someone who's worth extra time and effort. Here's how to do it:

Make a good first impression: Public defenders are used to assessing people very quickly—they have to be, because they often deal with dozens of clients every day. You may have only a few minutes to prove that *you* are a person who deserves special attention.

Be polite: One of the tougher aspects of being a public defender is that most of their clients are dubious about the public defender's skills and motives. In fact, some clients are downright rude. This is understandable, since most people aren't at their best when they've just been arrested, spent the night in jail, are facing criminal charges, and are stuck with a lawyer

they didn't get to choose. However, it won't help you to take it out on your public defender. You've got to make nice if you want the best service.

Show that you want to win: Because most criminal defendants feel helpless and confused, many of them end up appearing rather passive. And a client who seems not to care isn't likely to inspire his public defender. Whether you're looking for the best possible plea bargain, or hoping to win at trial, you need to demonstrate to your lawyer that you've got the energy it takes to do the job. Look earnest. Show that you've got both fighting spirit and self-control.

Dress conservatively: Your lawyer will be wondering whether you have good enough judgment to perform well at trial, and one indicator of this is what you wear to court (assuming you're not coming from jail). You should put together an extremely conservative outfit—the kind you'd see on a bank teller. Don't dress in casual clothes like baggy pants, jeans or t-shirts. Don't have on anything at all sexy. Women should wear only a minimum of jewelry and men shouldn't wear any. Leave out piercings other than earrings, and take off any removable tooth decorations, like gold fronts.[3]

Don't get drunk or high before court or meetings: Court hearings and meetings with lawyers are stressful, so sometimes people take the edge off their discomfort by self-medicating. Your lawyer will almost always be able to tell if you're in an altered state. And he's likely to feel that if you show up to a hearing or a meeting that way, then you must have a really severe substance abuse problem that would make it pretty hard to work closely with you or get through a trial successfully.

Help with the work: Most defendants don't do much to help themselves, so it may take your lawyer by surprise that you're ready to dig in and work on the case. If your lawyer's doing a good job, she'll explain what you can do to be of genuine assistance. Ask whether she'd like you to take on any of the following tasks:

- Create a list of potential witnesses (eye witnesses and character witnesses). Supply complete addresses, phone numbers, and background information about each individual, with good notes about what the witness can say on your behalf. (See sample witness list, page 171.)

---

1. This applies to most public defenders working in county or state courts. However, federal defenders, who represent low-income defendants in federal court, have fairly reasonable case loads and resources.

2. On the bright side, public defenders become quite familiar with the local judges and prosecutors, and can make very accurate predictions about how they'll behave.

3. This isn't meant to cramp your style or stifle your soul. If you're a criminal defendant, the courtroom is hostile ground—and in enemy territory, soldiers who want to survive wear camouflage.

- Make a time-line of what happened, with dates and times of day, as appropriate. (See sample time-line, page 172.)

- Draw diagrams of the scene of the incident, with actual measurements, if possible. (See sample diagram, page 173.)

- Set up an appointment to sit down with your lawyer and go over the police report page by page, looking for contradictions and lies.

- If drug or alcohol treatment would be useful to you, research local programs and interview with the ones that seem best. A letter of acceptance from a treatment center may be of great value in getting a good plea bargain.

- If you anticipate pleading guilty, especially to misdemeanor charges, look into non-profit agencies through which you might do community service. Get a letter from the organization saying that they'd really appreciate your help with a particular project or task.

If your lawyer doesn't look impressed by your first efforts at making a witness list, time-line, or similar notes, get her to tell you what has to be done to fix them. Write a second draft and show it to her again. This is a learning process—you're not expected to be great at it right from the start. Also, delivering a new (or revised) document to your attorney once a week is a good way to keep her focused on your case.

If you're not in jail, do whatever it takes to type your notes to your lawyer, instead of writing them by hand. He'll understand them faster and better that way. You want him to spend his time working on your case, not deciphering your handwriting.

Read over the section Having a Productive Meeting With Your Lawyer, page 170, and bring this book with you when you meet with your attorney. Ask questions and take notes. If your lawyer doesn't think the questions are relevant, find out what she feels you *should* be concentrating on.

Note: all of the above suggestions apply even if you've got a private attorney. You'll almost always be happier with the results when you work closely with your lawyer and take an active role in fighting your case.

HOW MUCH TO TELL YOUR LAWYER

Naturally, you want to give your lawyer as much information as possible, so that you get the best legal advice; but *how* you say it is critical.

Here's the problem: If you tell your lawyer the story of what happened, and then in court you tell a different story, it may appear that you've committed perjury (lied under oath). And if your lawyer knows you've committed perjury, he may be required to inform the judge or else immediately withdraw from the case (which in itself lets the judge know that you just committed perjury).[4]

Fortunately, you can avoid this conflict of interest by choosing your words carefully and being alert while talking to your lawyer:

1. Don't insist on telling your story right away—let your lawyer guide the conversation. Most lawyers have a mental outline of how they want to conduct the interview or meeting. Your lawyer will absorb your answers better if she gets the pieces of information in the order she has in mind. For example, many criminal defense lawyers like to start by going over the police report with you (so that you can respond to the accusations), before hearing your account of what happened.

2. Your lawyer may structure his questions very carefully, so that you can give him needed information without eliminating possible lines of argument. So listen to the exact wording of the question; answer it precisely; then stop. (Don't worry about giving too short an answer. If your lawyer needs to hear more, you can be quite sure he'll ask a follow-up question.)

3. When you ask questions or want to add information your lawyer hasn't asked for, do it in the form of a hypothetical question. The easy way to do this is to start your question with the words, "Hypothetically speaking…?"

4. If your lawyer interrupts you, try to figure out why. It could be that he's just being a jerk, but possibly he's trying to keep you from saying something that will limit your options later on.[5]

---

4. This is more of a problem for low-income people who are relying on a court-appointed lawyer, such as a public defender. Clients who've got enough money can always switch lawyers before trial, if they find they've over-shared.

   Although in general your lawyer must keep your secrets (see Maintaining Confidentiality, page 174), this does not apply if you lie while testifying. If it's discovered that a lawyer knew about a client's perjury and failed to report it, the lawyer could be disbarred (lose his license to practice law).

5. If you're not sure what your lawyer's up to, just ask: "Are you interrupting me because I'm starting to say something you don't need to hear, or is it for some other reason?"

In the cartoon above, the silly client admitted to his lawyer that he touched the car. So if that client testifies in court that he *didn't* touch the car, the lawyer may be required to snitch. The smart client answered his lawyer's question very precisely, giving his lawyer enough information to plan the defense strategy, without limiting his own testimony.

In the cartoon above, the silly client told her lawyer that she was selling marijuana. So if that client testifies in court that she didn't sell any of it, her lawyer may be required to snitch. The smart client did not officially tell her lawyer that she was selling marijuana. But she successfully alerted her lawyer to the matter a way that will allow them to discuss the legal issues involved.

HAVING A PRODUCTIVE MEETING WITH YOUR LAWYER

It often happens, when you're talking to a specialist such as a doctor or a lawyer, that you'll understand things during the conversation, but the next day it doesn't all quite make sense anymore or perhaps some of the details are missing. So, take notes when you're meeting with your lawyer and, at the end, go back over the key points with her. (This is also useful feedback for lawyers, because it tells them whether they're communicating clearly.)

The following are questions that may be relevant during your initial meetings with a criminal defense attorney.

- What are the charges against me at this point? Is the prosecutor likely to change the charges?

- What's the *maximum* sentence I'm facing (the worst case scenario)? What would be the *average* sentence for someone who went to trial and were convicted on these charges? I might choose to plead guilty, instead of going to trial, in exchange for lesser charges and/or a smaller punishment. Has the prosecutor offered a plea bargain? If there hasn't been an offer yet, what sort of plea bargain do think you I'm likely to get?

- Who is my judge and what can we expect from him or her? Are we going to have this judge for the whole case, or will we switch judges at some point?[6]

- Are there co-defendants in my case? If so, who are they? Would it better if my case were separated from theirs, and is that possible?

- Which elements of each charge do you think would be hard for the prosecutor to prove and why?

- Besides attacking the elements of the charges, what are some of the other defenses available to me? Are any of them contradictory, so that we have to choose some and give up others? At what point will we need to make a decision about this?

- What items of potential evidence are you asking the prosecution to give us, as part of the "discovery process?"

- What kinds of potential evidence does the defense need to locate? How can my friends and I help with the investigation?

- Whom are you thinking of calling as witnesses? I may be able to remember witnesses to the incident who would be helpful. And I may be able to find character witnesses for myself. How can I best help?

- What kinds of exhibits will we need in court? Photos, maps, diagrams? Is there anything my friends and I can do to help?

- What motions[7] have you made so far? What motions are you planning to make? Has the prosecutor made any motions? Has the judge ruled on any of the motions yet?

- Have any dates been set for filing or arguing [more] motions? How do I get copies of written motions in my case? Which motions do you think will be granted?

- At a maximum, if I want to be very involved in my case, what are the best ways for me to contact you and how often do you prefer to be contacted?

- If I want to look at some of the potential evidence in my case, such as police reports, when would be a good time?

- At a minimum, when do I have to be in town and in court?

- Is there anything else I should know about my case?

(And remember to say: "Thank you for all the work you're doing!")

---

6. In some court systems, you have the same judge from your very first appearance all the way through trial. In other court systems, you have separate judges for different stages of the case (an arraignment judge, a motions judge, a trial judge, etc.) It may also possible to "challenge" the judge, that is, get a different judge for your particular case.

7. Motions are requests to the judge, backed up by a discussion of points of law and the facts of the case. Motions can be oral or written. They often concern the evidence, witnesses or arguments to be used at trial.

CONFIDENTIAL ATTORNEY/CLIENT CORRESPONDENCE

243 Battery St.
Metropolis, WD 20535

April 1, 2003

Clara Darrow, Esq.
1886 Haymarket Sq.
Metropolis, WD 20535

        Re: <u>People v. Smith</u>, No. 03-647508

Dear Ms. Darrow:

    Here is my list of witnesses, so far. I divided it between
witnesses who were there during the incident, and witnesses who could
testify about my character.

Incident

Nora Choy   (202) 225-5074 home
32 Canal St.   (202) 224-1700 cell
Metropolis, WD 20510

Jamilia Queen   (202) 225-4121 home
247 Plate Blvd.   (202) 224-3871 cell
Metropolis, WD 20500   jam@hermajesty.net

Maria Florian   (202) 226-8417 home
Bridge Rd.   (202) 224-2981 cell
Metropolis, WD 20515

Joe Faith   (202) 225-4151
3637 Front St.
Metropolis, WD 20535

Character

Rev. Benedict Almworthy   (202) 226-7270 work
Church of the Holy Witness
120 High St.   Rev. Almworthy has known me since I
Metropolis, WD 20515   was a little kid.

Consuela Rodriguez   (202) 225-3621 work
Metropolitan Community College
500 4th St.   Connie's been my guidance counselor
Metropolis, WD 20510   for two years.

    There's some more witnesses to the incident, that I'm still tracking
down, but these are the ones I'm sure about at this point. Should I look
for more character witnesses, too?

                            Yours sincerely,

                            Chris Smith

                            Chris Smith

CONFIDENTIAL ATTORNEY/CLIENT CORRESPONDENCE

243 Battery St.
Metropolis, WD 20535

April 1, 2003

Clara Darrow, Esq.
1886 Haymarket Sq.
Metropolis, WD 20535

Re: People v. Smith, No. 03-647508

Dear Ms. Darrow:

Here's the first draft of my time line. I still need to look through
my calendar and loose papers, to figure out the exact dates for things that
happened farther back. Let me know where to put more detail.

9/02   Jada and Tamiko got into a lot of arguments, all month.
Eventually, they agreed to stay away from each other, after
Ms. Rodriguez had a meeting with both of them.

12/18?/02   Jada and Tamiko had a big verbal fight, right before the end
of the semester. Jamilia, Maria and I were there while they
were yelling at each other.

1/27/03

8:30 a.m.   Jada bumped into Tamiko on the way into our classroom. I was
there and so was Nora.

9:20 a.m.   During break, I went outside to get a soda from the vending
machines. When I was coming back, I saw Jada go up to Tamiko
and start yelling at her. Jada and Tamiko both looked mad.

9:22 a.m.   I went over to the two of them, to try and calm things down.
Since Tamiko's my friend, I spoke to her, saying "Come on,
let's just go. Don't even talk to her."

9:23 a.m.   Jada turned to me and yelled right in my face: "Stay the fuck
out of this, bitch!"

9:24 a.m.   Tamiko shoved Jada, yelling, "Don't you talk to her like
that! You got a problem, you fucking talk to me!"

9:25 a.m.   Jada slapped Tamiko across the face, right-handed.

9:26 a.m.   Tamiko grabbed a handful of Jada's hair - a bunch of her
extensions were pulled out, and maybe some of her hair, too.

9:27 a.m.   Jada was screaming non-stop. Both Jada and Tamiko were
hitting each other, mostly in the face, and calling each
other bitches and ho's and such.

9:28 a.m.   Campus security guards showed up - three men and a woman.
They broke up the fight and took Jada and Tamiko into
custody. Then they arrested me, too, because Jada claimed
that I hit her - which I didn't.

(continued)

CONFIDENTIAL ATTORNEY/CLIENT CORRESPONDENCE

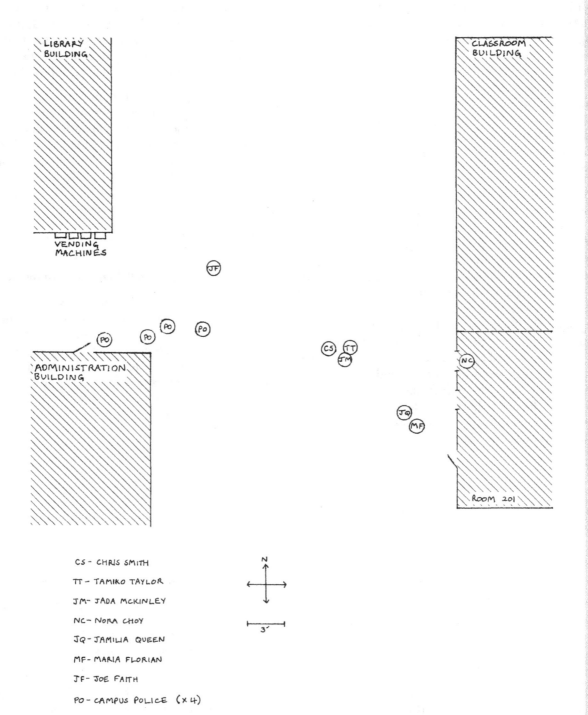

CS - CHRIS SMITH

TT - TAMIKO TAYLOR

JM - JADA MCKINLEY

NC - NORA CHOY

JQ - JAMILIA QUEEN

MF - MARIA FLORIAN

JF - JOE FAITH

PO - CAMPUS POLICE (X 4)

Your lawyer is required to keep your secrets, a legal doctrine referred to as "attorney/client privilege."[8] This means that you can speak freely, without worrying about your lawyer being called as a witness against you.[9] In addition, everyone who works with your lawyer is bound by the attorney/client privilege, including: other lawyers who are employed by the same office, investigators, interpreters, paralegals, and clerical staff. They're not allowed to share information about you, nor can they be subpoenaed. Also, a lawyer has to protect your confidentiality even if you don't hire him. You might speak with one attorney, talking about the details of your case, and then decide to hire a different lawyer. The first one has to keep your secrets, even though you're not working with him.

Unfortunately, it's easy to destroy attorney/client privilege if you're not extremely careful. Whatever you tell your lawyer is protected, but only if you don't tell other people. That means you can't share the details of your case with your family, friends, or bartender. Nor can they sit in on meetings between you and your attorney. Once the material is no longer private between you and your lawyer, it's no longer privileged. Anyone other than your lawyer and her staff can be subpoenaed—forced to testify against you or else be sent to jail for contempt. So for their sake, as well as yours, you've got to restrict what you say. Besides, word gets around and there may be someone out there who doesn't like you—a friend of a friend of a friend—who'd be perfectly happy to testify for the prosecution. So don't lose control of information that could conceivably hurt you in court.

Of course, you can tell other people when your hearings are, what you're charged with, and that you're not guilty. That's a matter of public record. But once you've said that much, you have to stop. An easy way to do this is to say:

I'm sorry, but my lawyer says I can't talk about the case, not even with my family and closest friends. But it means a lot to me to know that you're on my side. I hope you can come to court and show that there're people who believe in me.

Now, it may happen that certain family members or friends might be good witnesses on your behalf. To include them in the case, you should first discuss with your lawyer what these potential witnesses could testify about. If your lawyer thinks they'll be helpful, she or her staff will talk to them directly. This conversation—between the witness and the lawyer—will then be protected (by the "attorney work product rule").

Whenever you write notes or letters to your lawyer, at the top of the page put:

Confidential Attorney/Client Correspondence

If you're writing from jail, put it on the outside of the envelope, too. And remember, jail phones are not private—the authorities can listen in—so what you say to your lawyer on a jail phone is not protected by the attorney/client privilege. If you're in jail, wait until your lawyer visits you in person before disclosing any private information.

---

8. Of course, there are exceptions. Your lawyer is required to tell the judge or withdraw from the case if he knows you've committed perjury (see How Much to Tell Your Lawyer, page 168). Also, if you tell your lawyer—seriously—that you're planning to injure someone, the lawyer may be required to inform the police (so avoid stupid jokes). Finally, if your lawyer ends up in litigation with you, he's allowed to testify. For example, if you sue your lawyer, or if your lawyer becomes your co-defendant in a criminal case, the lawyer is entitled to testify about things you've said or shown to him.

9. There are a few other privileges, similar to the attorney/client privilege. For example, the priest/penitent privilege prohibits religious professionals (priests, ministers, rabbis and imams) from testifying about matters you've confided to them. And in most jurisdictions, the doctor/patient privilege prevents medical professionals (doctors and psychotherapists, as well as the nurses and other staff who work with them) from testifying about what you've said as a patient. However, there isn't a privilege that relates to journalists. A reporter or photographer can be subpoenaed, along with her notes, photos, tapes, film, etc. Some states have passed "shield laws," that allow professional journalists to withhold the identity of a source (though not the information provided by the source), but a judge may still choose to compel disclosure.

REPRESENTING YOURSELF

A defendant who represents herself is referred to as proceeding *pro se* or *in pro per*.[10] You have the right to represent yourself, provided that the judge decides you're "competent" (that you have enough experience and education to manage it).[11] You needn't have taken courses in law or be familiar with technical matters such as hearsay exceptions, to exercise your right to self-representation. However, you do have to understand the basic procedures undertaken by the defense and the prosecution:

- Each side gets to make an opening statement at the beginning of trial and a closing argument at its end.

- Each side can put on witnesses and items of physical evidence, and use subpoenas to force them to appear, if necessary.

- Each side can cross-examine the other side's witnesses.

- Each side can object to testimony or exhibits on the basis of the rules of evidence, and the judge will then decide whether the material in question may be presented to the jury.

- The prosecutor usually makes the first opening statement and the last closing argument, and normally puts on all of her witnesses and exhibits before the defense puts on any.

- Each side is responsible for submitting a set of jury instructions.

The judge is required to verify that you're familiar with how a trial works. He also has to confirm that you know you're entitled to a court-appointed lawyer if you can't afford one. Usually, the judge will start by warning you about the dangers of representing yourself. Then he'll ask about your level of education, ability to speak English, whether you've ever been through a criminal trial before, etc. This conversation between you and the judge is called a *"Faretta* hearing."[12] It's rarely a separate proceeding; instead, it occurs at whatever point you tell the judge that you're planning to represent yourself. Sometimes judges are pretty disrespectful during the *Faretta* hearing, especially when they're talking about

how unwise it would be for you to represent yourself.[13] However, if you lose your temper in response (especially if you yell or swear), the judge will most definitely declare that you're not competent to represent yourself. If the judge does decide you're not competent, he'll appoint a lawyer to represent you despite your wishes.

Since the legal profession is an elitist monopoly, the drawbacks to representing yourself are huge. The judge and prosecutor won't give you any breaks, even though you haven't been to law school. If you can't make or oppose objections, introduce evidence correctly, or handle complex motions, no one will help you. And most people who represent themselves just look foolish to the judge and jury, especially if they stumble over legal jargon or speak pompously. (Lawyers aren't very well liked in our society; but a wannabe who pretentiously poses as a lawyer is liked even less.) Some judges will mock you when you make mistakes. And other judges will be friendly and polite, and sit there watching while you walk right into the prosecutor's traps. The fact that the judge has declared you competent doesn't mean he thinks you really are able to defend yourself adequately—the *Faretta* hearing is just a requirement the judge has to fulfill to avoid grounds for appeal. (Judges find it embarrassing when their cases are overturned because they made a procedural mistake.) To sum up, it's a lousy idea to represent yourself, especially if you're stuck in jail before or during trial. Even a bad lawyer is likely to know more about how to write motions and make objections than someone who isn't licensed to practice law. So, if your lawyer's not satisfactory and you can't afford to get a different one, your best bet is probably to assist your lawyer with whatever tasks you're capable of doing (research, investigation, preparing exhibits, locating witnesses, etc.).

The one type of criminal matter in which it can be worthwhile to represent yourself is a case involving political activism (such as civil disobedience)—especially when the charges are misdemeanors and the amount of potential jail time is thus more limited. In political cases, judges often forbid defendants to talk about the reasons—philosophical or religious—for their actions. Such defendants may have a better chance of getting the

---

10. *Pro se* is a Latin expression that means, "on one's own behalf." *In pro per* is an abbreviation of the Latin phrase *in propria persona*, which means "in one's own person"; that is, speaking oneself instead of talking through a representative. The expression *pro se* is used in federal court and in some state courts; other state courts use *in pro per*.

11. Don't confuse being competent to represent yourself with being competent to stand trial. Competence to represent yourself requires familiarity with the mechanics of a criminal trial. Competence to stand trial merely requires sanity.

12. Some courts use a written form, covering the questions usually asked during a *Faretta* hearing. To represent yourself, you'll be required to sign the form, agreeing to all the statements on it.

13. Judges occasionally recite: "The defendant who represents himself has a fool for a lawyer," among other helpful remarks.

message across if they represent themselves. Although a political defendant who represents herself is nonetheless more likely to lose the case than if she uses a lawyer, she may find the trial more satisfying. Anyway, if it's clear that it's impossible to win, then a political defendant has nothing to lose by representing herself—and speaking truth to power in the courtroom is itself an important form of activism. For inspiration, you might look at court statements by people such as Socrates, William Penn, Emma Goldman, Mohandas K. Gandhi, Dorothy Day, and Nelson Mandela.[14] If you're going to do time anyway, you might as well have your say.

A middle ground between having a lawyer do everything and representing yourself alone, is to have a lawyer as "advisory counsel" or "co-counsel."[15] The precise range of activities for advisory counsel or co-counsel to a *pro se* defendant varies according to the preferences of individual trial judges, so the following descriptions are just generalizations.

> **Advisory Counsel:** a lawyer who writes and argues motions, and stays in the courtroom during trial (either in the audience or at the defense table). Advisory counsel doesn't speak in front of the jury, but can usually help with legal arguments to the judge, when the jury can't hear. The defendant can pause periodically to get help from the advisory counsel, especially about procedural issues.

> **Co-Counsel to a Pro Se Defendant:** a lawyer who can write and argue motions, and speak to the jury and witnesses. Co-counsel sits with the defendant and they work as a team. This is sometimes referred to as "hybrid representation."

Having advisory counsel is awkward for the defendant, because it's often difficult to stop in the middle of things to ask questions. Sometimes judges appoint advisory counsel whether the defendant wants it or not—particularly if the judge thinks she may want to declare the defendant incompetent at some point in the middle of the proceedings, and order the advisory counsel to take over representing the defendant.

A *pro se* defendant with co-counsel has an advantage, in that the lawyer can do technical tasks, like making objections and cross-examining prosecution witnesses; while the defendant can do things like examine defense witnesses, or give the opening statement or closing argument. Judges are often resistant to allowing hybrid rep-

resentation, but can sometimes be convinced if they're assured that the lawyer and the defendant will figure out in advance exactly who's going to do what, so they won't be interrupting or talking over each other.

FIRING YOUR LAWYER

First off, before you give up on your lawyer altogether, try writing him a letter, explaining the problems you're having with him. A formal communication of this sort may get his attention. Bear in mind that clients and lawyers frequently get frustrated with each other right before and during trial (when both client and lawyer are anxious and irritable)—and this type of friction can often be worked out.

When it does become necessary, it's pretty easy to dump your lawyer. You can just say: "You're fired," or words to that effect. However, if your lawyer has come to court on your behalf and "made a general appearance" (gone on record as your lawyer), then she has to get the judge's permission to withdraw from your case. And the judge will want whoever's taking over to "substitute in as the new attorney of record."

If you're just switching from one private attorney to a different private attorney, the lawyers themselves will handle the paperwork.

If you're firing your attorney and planning to represent yourself, then the judge has to hold a *Faretta* hearing to decide whether you're competent to do so (see Representing Yourself, page 175).

If you've got a public defender whom you don't like, it can be difficult to get a different court-appointed lawyer. First, you should try talking to your attorney's supervisor about it. Even if you're not given a new lawyer, the one you've got may work harder, knowing that the supervisor is paying attention. If this is not satisfactory, you can ask the judge to appoint a different attorney, but judges are reluctant to do so, particularly if you're close to trial. You may have to convince the judge that your public defender has behaved really inappropriately or else completely ignored you, and there's no way you can work together effectively. It will help if you keep a list of your lawyer's offensive or inadequate actions and statements, and write letters to your lawyer describing the problem you're having with him (keep copies, of course).

---

14. There's a collection of statements made by activists during court proceedings on the Just Cause Law Collective website: http://www.lawcollective.org/.

15. Co-counsel normally just means any lawyer in a case with more than one attorney on the same side (for example: a case with multiple defendants each of whom has a lawyer; or one defendant with a team of lawyers). In this context, it means a lawyer who is helping represent a *pro se* defendant.

If you change lawyers, it will almost always delay your case. The new lawyer will want to ask the judge for a continuance (extension), in order to digest all the information in the case and undertake tasks that the old lawyer didn't do.

If you fire a privately retained lawyer, you don't necessarily get any of your money back. Most fee agreements state that the fee is non-refundable. If you're parting from your lawyer on reasonably friendly terms and she hasn't done much work yet, you may be able to negotiate a partial refund—but don't count on it.

If you've fired your lawyer, he's required to give a copy of the file he created for your case to the new lawyer (or to you, if you're representing yourself). It's illegal for an attorney to hold the file hostage, even if you owe him money.

SUING YOUR LAWYER

Suing your lawyer is tough. The legal system is run by lawyers and by judges (who used to be lawyers), so they tend to take the attorney's side. To win, you'll need a lawyer who has expertise in "attorney malpractice" litigation. Malpractice suits against lawyers tend to be based on mishandling money, negligence, missed deadlines, conflict of interest, or sexual harassment. If this is going on in your case, be sure to document it thoroughly.

If it's not feasible to sue your lawyer, you may want to file a complaint with his state bar association. This may or may not result in any disciplinary action, but at least your statement will be kept on file and may help some other client in the future prove that this attorney has a consistent pattern of misbehavior.

APPENDICES

Walker, Samuel, Miriam Delone, and Cassia C. Spohn. *The Color of Justice: Race, Ethnicity, and Crime in America,* 3d ed. Belmont, CA: Wadsworth, 2003.

Extremely well organized. Provides the definitions and statistics you need to have a useful discussion of inequities in the legal system. Covers police, court, prison, and the death penalty. Includes convenient overviews of studies and theories on discrimination in criminal justice. (315 pages)

Mauer, Marc. *Race to Incarcerate: The Sentencing Project.* New York: New Press, 1999.

Investigates race and class in the context of prison. Examines the "Tough on Crime" Movement and the War on Drugs. Also brief but useful discussion of news coverage concerning crime and incarceration. (194 pages)

The Sentencing Project: http://www.sentencingproject.org/.

Various reports analyzing disparate treatment in sentencing on the basis of race, class, and gender. Also short "fact sheets," useful for overviews or quick research.

Building Blocks for Youth: http://www.buildingblocksforyouth.org/.

Contains and cites many studies on minority youth in the justice system. Some studies concern the treatment of young women, and the report *¿Dónde está la Justicia?* relates to Latino youth.

Harris, David. *Profiles in Injustice: Why Racial Profiling Cannot Work.* New York: New Press, 2002.

Everything you need to know about racial profiling: history, important court cases, and statistical studies. Moving descriptions of the impact of racial profiling on individuals, along with explanations of its unconstitutionality, and its ineffectiveness as a law enforcement technique. (227 pages)

Berry, Mary F. *The Pig Farmer's Daughter and Other Tales of American Justice: Episodes of Racism and Sexism in the Courts from 1865 to the Present.* New York: Knopf, 1999.

Stories showing the effects of sexism and racism in court cases, both during trial and on appeal. Includes cases involving extramarital sex, gay and lesbian relationships, prostitution, seduction, child support, abortion, rape, and incest. (243 pages)

Miller, Jerome G. *Search and Destroy: African-American Males in the Criminal Justice System.* New York: Cambridge University Press, 1996.

Fairly intellectual analysis of racism in the legal system, but full of graphic accounts of official mistreatment and the horrifying complacency of those who condone it. (242 pages)

Reiman, Jeffrey. *The Rich Get Richer and the Poor Get Prison: Ideology, Class and Criminal Justice.* New York: Macmillan, 1990.

Very lively presentation on the nature of crime, and how class and race influence who is punished. Reminiscent of Michael Moore (director of *TV Nation, Bowling for Columbine,* etc.), but with an explicitly Marxist slant. (178 pages)

Leonard, Kimberly K., C. Pope, and W. Feversherm, eds. *Minorities in Juvenile Justice.* Thousand Oaks, CA: Sage, 1995.

To understand every word of these articles, you'd need to have taken a class in statistics (and still remember some of it), but most of the tables and discussions are pretty clear. Chapters 2 and 7 summarize interviews with police, prosecutors, public defenders and judges, exposing their attitudes concerning race and class. (216 pages)

There's a great deal of reference material on discrimination in the legal system and on police misconduct (the subject of Appendix B). I looked at about 50 books and selected the ones mentioned here because they were easy to find in public libraries, up-to-date, and for the most part reasonable to read (not written for the edification of other academicians). They're listed in order of how useful and readable they seemed to me. The number of pages listed for each book is generally just the text, not the notes, indices, bibliographies, etc.

Lynch, Michael and E. Britt Patterson, eds. *Justice With Prejudice: Race and Criminal Justice in America.* Albany, NY: Harrow and Heston, 1996.

   A collection of rather academic articles, but Chapter 5 provides important statistics and analysis on racism in media coverage of crime. (169 pages)

Up to date statistics on law enforcement, conviction, and sentencing can be obtained online. Good websites include:

   Bureau of Justice Statistics (BJS)
   http://www.ojp.usdoj.gov/bjs/

   National Criminal Justice Reference Service (NCJRS)
   http://www.ncjrs.org/

   Sourcebook of criminal justice statistics Online (SCJS)
   http://www.albany.edu/sourcebook/

However, the data is often presented in such a way that it's hard to spot the instances of systemic discrimination. You may have to draw on several different tables and do a little math to get useful information. Before you start number-crunching, read some of the books listed above to see how they analyzed the statistical material, because you may want to follow their approach. The agencies that publish these statistics have staff who can help you find the right data, especially if you explain really clearly what you're after. Check the websites to get up-to-date contact information (including 800 numbers)—look under "Contact" for BJS and NCJRS, and under "About Sourcebook" for SCJS.

American Civil Liberties Union. *Fighting Police Abuse: A Community Action Manual.* New York: ACLU, 1997.

> Profiles of various community groups that combat police misconduct, demonstrating different strategies: video camera patrols, lawsuits, lobbying, etc. Which statistics are useful and which are misleading. How to start or improve a police review organization. Good bibliography and list of contacts. (54 pages)

Ogletree, Charles et al. *Beyond the Rodney King Story: An Investigation of Police Conduct in Minority Communities.* Boston: Northeastern University Press, 1995.

> Very well organized presentation of the results of an NAACP study. Analysis of the types and causes of police misconduct, followed by an array of recommendations on how to stop it. (198 pages)

Human Rights Watch Staff, *Shielded from Justice: Police Brutality and Accountability in the United States.* Human Rights Watch, 1998. (450 pages) (This report can also be viewed or downloaded at http://www.hrw.org/reports98/police/.)

> Detailed examination of police misconduct in 14 U.S. cities from 1995–1998. How investigations of misconduct can be thwarted at various stages. Extensive recommendations for reform.

Bernards, Neal. *Police Brutality: Recognizing Stereotypes.* San Diego: Greenhaven Press, 1994.

> Well designed lesson in spotting assumptions and rhetoric. Uses marginal notes and follow-up exercises to analyze contrasting viewpoints on police misconduct. Young adult level. (36 pages)

Kennedy, Adam and Adrienne Kennedy. *Sleep Deprivation Chamber: A Play.* New York: Theatre Communications Group, 1996.

> Powerful play about an African-American student who is arrested and beaten up by the police. He is falsely charged with assault and battery on an officer, and goes to trial. Many very realistic sequences in which witnesses are rigorously cross-examined about minute details. *If you expect to be a witness in a police misconduct case, read this to prepare yourself for testifying in court.* (72 pages)

Skolnick, Jerome and James Fyfe. *Above the Law: Police and the Excessive Use of Force.* New York: The Free Press, 1993.

> History and psychology of police misconduct. Analysis of strategies for controlling police misconduct. (313 pages)

If you have to go to jail, don't make yourself crazy remembering all the prison movies you've ever seen. Being put in the slammer is a lot like starting at a new high school: it's not that tough, as long as you pay attention from the outset and think about what kind of impression you're making.

The following are guidelines for getting along in jail:

- Watch and listen for quite a while, to get a sense of the other people you'll be living with. Really take your time about this, because you're likely to be dealing with different types of people than you're used to, and it's important to be accurate in your assessments. Some will be very decent human beings who can give you useful information and advice. On the other hand, the first ones who come up and want to make friends with you may be predators, losers, or snitches. Don't be in a big hurry to join a group, because you'll be taking on their baggage. Just take it easy and be pleasant with everyone, without striving to find buddies right away. Take the time to let friendships develop gradually, the way they do naturally at work, school, or the gym.

- Respect others, but behave with self-respect, too. Acting scared invites bullying. And if you don't stand up for yourself, potential allies won't think it's worth the risk to stand by you.

- Be very careful not to touch people by accident. If you do bump into anyone, immediately say "Excuse me." If your apology isn't accepted, don't argue, but just walk away (and keep an eye on that person for future problems).

- Don't touch other people's stuff (books, pencils, etc.) or sit on other people's beds, without asking.

- Rather than just joining a conversation, wait until someone asks your opinion. However bad your situation is, be careful not to sound like you're whining.

- In the eating area, don't reach across other people's trays. If you have to cough or sneeze, turn away and cover your mouth.

- Before using the telephone or changing channels on the TV, make sure you check with other prisoners to see what system they've set up for taking turns—it's easy to offend others by accident, if you don't find out the "local rules."

- Don't borrow money, don't gamble, don't do drugs, and don't accept gifts from strangers. All these things can put you in debt, which could affect your safety.

- Don't snitch. Snitches are not just unpopular—they're unsafe. Don't even refer to other prisoners when talking with correctional officers, because people will think you're snitching or at least being manipulated by the officers. (The primary exception to this is that if you honestly believe you're going to be raped, you may ask to be placed in protective custody.)

While forcible rape in jail or prison is infrequent, consensual sex is very common (although it's illegal and results in disciplinary action if you're caught). Lots of prisoners have sex with each other because doing time is boring and having sex is nice.[1]

Some prisoners agree to have sex because they're scared or in debt, though this mostly applies to male prisoners. Women in jail rarely get into physical fights or coerce each other into having sex, whereas men in jail are more likely to do both. Of course, conditions vary quite a bit from one institution to another—some places are mellow and some aren't. In any case, if you're propositioned and you're not interested in sex, just say no clearly, without freaking out (the same as you would in a bar). If your refusal isn't taken seriously, fight back (and sometimes just looking like you're ready to fight is enough). If you can't defend yourself, ask to be put in protective custody. Remember, however, that prisoners in protective custody are considered to be snitches, which means that it will be difficult ever to re-enter the institution's general population.

In just about every correctional institution that houses women, there are male officers who seduce female prisoners. Women in custody should stay away from over-friendly corrections officers—whatever they're offering (affection, money, or candy) is rarely worth the complications (pregnancy, sexually-transmitted diseases, and additional criminal charges).

If you have medical needs or disabilities, tell the staff. You'll probably have to make repeated requests, and you should keep copies of all written ones.

---

1. Some people who have same-gender sex partners in jail, but not when they're free, consider themselves straight. If you find yourself discussing the matter, be tactful.

On Doing Time: Excerpts of a letter from Erskine Johnson (Ndume Olatushani)[2]

There isn't a "one size fits all" solution; however, there are some simple things everyone can do to avoid most of the worst problems that go on in jails and prisons. Having said this, even the tried and true techniques may be severely tested, because there's always going to be some damn fool who's determined to make your life difficult.

I have to disagree with the statement, "No amount of good advice can help someone who's hopelessly weak or geeky." The fact of the matter is that even the weak and geeky can make it, as I have witnessed. One of the refuges for these guys is the church crowd. Of course, this isn't a guarantee, but it will make them less of a target if they walk around singing the praises of the Lord. There seems to be an unspoken code that convicts recognize: leave the Bible-toters alone. But it has to be real—the other prisoners will know if they're just faking it.

The first and most important piece of advice I'd give anyone entering jail or prison is: be yourself. Do not have an attitude, as there are many of us that will adjust attitudes. Being in a controlled environment allows people to observe you up close and personal. If you're putting up a front, they'll be able to sense your phoniness. They'll have no respect for you, and this can be an invitation for someone to try you.

If you are sent to prison, you'll likely have spent time in jail first. You should be keenly aware that how you conduct yourself in jail is going to follow you through the system. Because if you're in jail for any extended amount of time, you're going to see many of the same individuals later in prison. So if a guy is punked [sexually exploited] in the county jail, it will most likely continue throughout his prison bit (unless he attacks the first person that messes with him—the surest way to redeem oneself).

Believe it or not, playing is probably more responsible for people running afoul of each other than anything else. This is true for both verbal and physical play. So much trouble can be avoided by simply not playing with people. And when I say verbal play, I'm talking, for example, about "playing the dozen" [exchanging insults]. Physical play is often used as a pretext for more aggressive behavior. I've seen a prisoner turn a seemingly innocent game of wrestling into an opportunity to "turn out" [sexually exploit] the other guy, because through that wrestling game he was able to test this guy's resolve. But there are many more people hurt by verbal play than by any other forms of play. There is a large percentage of guys locked up who suffer from low self-esteem. So when people talk about them, even in fun, their feelings are easily hurt. If they cannot match their tormenters verbally, they usually resort to physical confrontation. My advice is: do not sit around laughing at jokes people make at the expense of others' feelings. Because I assure you, some one is going to eventually ask you "What are you laughing at?" And it's going to be on.

I've seen many guys come into jail or prison talking about whom they know or who their family is. And when you don't know the people you're talking to, this is not a wise thing to do. I witnessed a man killed like this, not to mention numerous people seriously hurt. One guy was bragging about how he'd shot a particular person. (He hadn't really shot him, but was just a buddy of the guy who'd done the shooting, and he only knew the victim by name.) It turned out that the victim was sitting only a few feet away from the guy who was telling the story. It ended with this guy getting severely beaten, all because he was pretending to be someone that he was not.

Avoid people that always want to sit around and talk about others. Most guys know who these people are, and you don't want to get a rap by association. And secondly, if such a person talks to you about others, at some point he'll talk to others about you.

Another big mistake that guys make in the joint is showing photographs of their family and friends to people they don't know. Trying to impress guys in this way can get you into trouble. I've seen people get hurt because they didn't realize they had enemies by virtue of association. And but for their showing photos, their difficulties might have been avoided.

Never talk about other crimes you've done on the streets. If other people start trying to tell you about unlawful things they've done, just say that they're telling you more than you need to know. This is also true for the illegal things that go on inside the joint. If it's not your business, tell the individual you don't need to know about that. If you're around other prisoners who start discussing activities that might get them in trouble, tell them you're going to cut out. This way, if it should come to light, you won't be accused of telling, because they'll

---

2. Mr. Erskine Johnson (Ndume Olatushani) was wrongfully convicted of murder in 1985. To learn more about his case and to obtain up-to-date information on how to write to Mr. Johnson, contact the Erskine Johnson Defense Committee, P.O. Box 68094, Nashville, TN 37206. The telephone number is (615) 228-4010.

APPENDIX C | ADVICE FOR THOSE GOING TO JAIL FOR THE FIRST TIME

already know you weren't in on it. And if you see other guys talking, don't walk up without knowing that it's all right to do so. If you're around others and they begin to whisper, make sure that you get out of earshot.

And last, but surely not least, develop a reputation for being your own man. Avoid taking sides if you can. And know the difference between "socializing" and "associating." It's all right to socialize with almost everyone, but you should limit the people with whom you associate, because their problems become your problems. And even though some of the most loyal people I know are right here in prison with me, I'm always mindful that people rarely will do for you what you will for them, whether one is locked up or in Freedomville.

GLOSSARY

Note: While some of the words below have additional meanings, the definitions given here relate only to criminal law.

arraignment. A short hearing at the beginning of a criminal case, at which the charges are announced and the defendant is asked to enter a plea (guilty, no contest, or not guilty).

bail. Money paid to the court, to get a defendant released from jail while a case is in progress. If the defendant shows up for court hearings and other legal commitments, the bail money is eventually given back. If the defendant runs away, the court gets to keep the bail money. When a defendant cannot pay the entire amount of bail, he may be able to get a loan through a bail bondsman, but the fee for this service is 10% of the total amount of bail—and that fee is *not* given back.

citation. An order to come to court, to face criminal charges. Traffic tickets are one type of citation.

deferred prosecution. A deal in which the prosecutor agrees to put a case "on hold" for a given period of time (usually six to eighteen months). As long as the defendant meets whatever conditions are imposed (similar to informal probation), the prosecutor will dismiss the case when the time is up. Deferred prosecution is only offered for minor crimes.

detention. A brief period in which a suspect is not free to go, while law enforcement officers investigate and decide whether they have enough proof to arrest the suspect. During detention, the suspect can be pat searched. (See reasonable suspicion; see also probable cause.)

diversion. A deal in which the defendant must meet certain conditions (similar to probation), after which the case is dismissed. Diversion is generally offered only once, the first time a defendant is brought to court on criminal charges, and only for minor crimes or drug cases. Some counties have special diversion programs for people arrested for prostitution, graffiti, or drugs.

entrapment. A defense to criminal charges, in which the defendant must prove both: (1) he had no tendency or desire to commit the crime, and (2) an undercover officer or informant intensely pressured him into doing it.

frisk. See pat search.

felony. A serious crime for which the punishment can include a year or more in prison.

green card. A permanent resident card, form I-551. A permanent resident is an immigrant who has permission to live and work in the United States permanently, but has not become a naturalized U.S. citizen and is therefore still subject to expulsion.

infraction. A very small crime, in most jurisdictions punishable only by a fine, rather than by jail time.

jail. A place where people are incarcerated *before* guilt or innocence has been determined (often because they can't afford bail); and also where people serve short sentences, usually less than a year, as punishment for misdemeanors or for violations of probation or parole. (Compare with prison.)

***Miranda* rights.** The warnings read to an arrested person whom the officers want to question: "You have the right to remain silent. Anything you say may be used against you in a court of law. You have the right to an attorney. If you cannot afford an attorney, one will be appointed for you by the court."

misdemeanor. A small crime, usually punishable by no more than a year in jail.

no contest. (In Latin, *nolo contendere*.) A plea to criminal charges, similar to pleading guilty. Pleading no contest, rather than guilty, may be of benefit if the defendant is sued in civil court, as well as being prosecuted criminally. However, a defendant who pleads no contest will be sentenced just as though he'd pleaded guilty.

parole. A form of court supervision, following release from state prison.

pat search. A search in which the officer runs his hands over the suspect's body, to check for weapons. The suspect remains clothed during a pat search.

plea bargain. An agreement with the prosecutor in which the defendant pleads guilty or no contest (thereby giving up his right to a trial), in exchange for a lesser charge and/or a smaller punishment.

prison. A place where convicted felons are incarcerated, usually for sentences longer than a year. Same as a penitentiary. (Compare with jail.)

probable cause. Enough proof of criminal activity for a law enforcement officer to arrest a suspect or get a search warrant. For example, a cop would have probable cause to arrest a suspect for felony vandalism if:

> A store owner calls the police department and describes someone who just spray-painted huge amounts of graffiti all over the front of his store. Officers are sent to the area and they notice a person who fits this description, running down the street about a block from the store, clutching a can of spray paint in his hand.

probation. A type of court supervision instead of, or in addition to, a jail term. Formal probation conditions may include:

> reporting regularly to a supervising officer
> obeying all laws
> restrictions on where you can go
> restrictions on whom you can see
> drug testing
> attendance at classes, counseling or meetings
> submission to searches without probable cause
> payment of fines and/or restitution

Informal probation conditions may include any of the above, other than reporting to a supervising officer.

promise to appear. An agreement to come to court, which an arrested person signs when being released from custody.

pro per. A defendant who's representing herself in court. Also called *pro se.*

release on recognizance. When the judge releases an arrested person from jail and, instead of requiring bail, relies only on the defendant's promise to come to court. Also called "ROR," "OR," or "PR."

reasonable suspicion. Enough proof of criminal activity for a law enforcement officer to detain a suspect (see detention). Also called "articulable suspicion," because the officer has to be able to articulate his reasons. For example, a cop would have reasonable suspicion if he said to himself:

> Hmmm, that guy keeps looking in the window of the jewelry store, then walking away, then coming back and peering into the store again. He's not from this neighborhood and he seems kind of nervous. Maybe he's planning a burglary.

subpoena. An order to appear as a witness, in court or before a grand jury. A subpoena *duces tecum* is an order to appear and bring particular items with you (such as documents or possessions).

waiver. Giving up a legal right.

wingspan. The searchable area around an arrested suspect—as large as the distance the suspect could leap to in any direction.

INDEX

Don't forget to look in the Glossary for definitions (page 186).

References to footnotes look like this: 28n7 [page 28, note 7].

ABOUT THE AUTHOR AND ILLUSTRATOR

Author: Katya Komisaruk was sentenced to five years in federal prison following a protest against nuclear weapons in 1987. From behind bars, Katya applied to law school. She graduated *cum laude* from Harvard Law School in 1993, and went into practice focusing on criminal defense and civil rights. In 1999, Katya began working with activists and attorneys across the country to develop legal strategies to protect citizens' civil rights during large-scale demonstrations. She is now a lawyer with the Just Cause Law Collective, based in Oakland, California, providing legal representation and workshops to individuals and community groups.

Illustrator: Tim Maloney is a rather private person. He draws pictures.

Books

MARTHA ACKELSBERG—*Free Women of Spain*

KATHY ACKER—*Pussycat Fever*

MICHAEL ALBERT—*Moving Forward: Program for a Participatory Economy*

JOEL ANDREAS—*Addicted to War: Why the U.S. Can't Kick Militarism*

ALEXANDER BERKMAN—*What is Anarchism?*

HAKIM BEY—*Immediatism*

JANET BIEHL & PETER STAUDENMAIER—*Ecofascism: Lessons From The German Experience*

BIOTIC BAKING BRIGADE—*Pie Any Means Necessary: The Biotic Baking Brigade Cookbook*

JACK BLACK—*You Can't Win*

MURRAY BOOKCHIN—*Anarchism, Marxism, and the Future of the Left*

MURRAY BOOKCHIN—*Social Anarchism or Lifestyle Anarchism: An Unbridgeable Chasm*

MURRAY BOOKCHIN—*Spanish Anarchists: The Heroic Years 1868–1936, The*

MURRAY BOOKCHIN—*To Remember Spain: The Anarchist and Syndicalist Revolution of 1936*

MURRAY BOOKCHIN—*Which Way for the Ecology Movement?*

DANNY BURNS—*Poll Tax Rebellion*

CHRIS CARLSSON—*Critical Mass: Bicycling's Defiant Celebration*

JAMES CARR–*Bad*

NOAM CHOMSKY—*At War With Asia*

NOAM CHOMSKY—*Language and Politics*

NOAM CHOMSKY—*Radical Priorities*

WARD CHURCHILL—*On the Justice of Roosting Chickens: Reflections on the Consequences of U.S. Imperial Arrogance and Criminality*

HARRY CLEAVER—*Reading Capital Politically*

ALEXANDER COCKBURN & JEFFREY ST. CLAIR (ed.)—*Politics of Anti-Semitism, The*

ALEXANDER COCKBURN & JEFFREY ST. CLAIR (ed.)—*Serpents in the Garden*

DANIEL & GABRIEL COHN-BENDIT—*Obsolete Communism: The Left-Wing Alternative*

EG SMITH COLLECTIVE—*Animal Ingredients A–Z (3rd edition)*

VOLTAIRINE de CLEYRE—*Voltarine de Cleyre Reader*

HOWARD EHRLICH—*Reinventing Anarchy, Again*

SIMON FORD—*Realization And Suppression Of The Situationist International: An Annotated Bibliography 1972–1992, The*

YVES FREMION & VOLNY—*Orgasms of History: 3000 Years of Spontaneous Revolt*

DANIEL GUERIN—*No Gods No Masters*

AGUSTIN GUILLAMON—*Friends Of Durruti Group, 1937–1939, The*

ANN HANSEN—*Direct Action: Memoirs Of An Urban Guerilla*

WILLIAM HERRICK—*Jumping the Line: The Adventures and Misadventures of an American Radical*

FRED HO—*Legacy to Liberation: Politics & Culture of Revolutionary Asian/Pacific America*

STEWART HOME—*Assault on Culture*

STEWART HOME—*Neoism, Plagiarism & Praxis*

STEWART HOME—*Neoist Manifestos / The Art Strike Papers*

STEWART HOME—*No Pity*

STEWART HOME—*Red London*

STEWART HOME—*What Is Situationism? A Reader*

JAMES KELMAN—*Some Recent Attacks: Essays Cultural And Political*

KEN KNABB—*Complete Cinematic Works of Guy Debord*

NESTOR MAKHNO—*Struggle Against The State & Other Essays, The*

G.A. MATIASZ—*End Time*

CHERIE MATRIX—*Tales From the Clit*

ALBERT MELTZER—*Anarchism: Arguments For & Against*

ALBERT MELTZER—*I Couldn't Paint Golden Angels*

RAY MURPHY—*Siege Of Gresham*

NORMAN NAWROCKI—*Rebel Moon*

HENRY NORMAL—*Map of Heaven, A*

HENRY NORMAL—*Dream Ticket*

HENRY NORMAL—*Fifteenth of February*

HENRY NORMAL—*Third Person*

FIONBARRA O'DOCHARTAIGH—*Ulster's White Negroes: From Civil Rights To Insurrection*

DAN O'MAHONY—*Four Letter World*

CRAIG O'HARA—*Philosophy Of Punk, The*

ANTON PANNEKOEK—*Workers' Councils*

BEN REITMAN—*Sister of the Road: the Autobiography of Boxcar Bertha*

PENNY RIMBAUD—*Diamond Signature, The*

PENNY RIMBAUD—*Shibboleth: My Revolting Life*

RUDOLF ROCKER—*Anarcho-Syndicalism*

RON SAKOLSKY & STEPHEN DUNIFER—*Seizing the Airwaves: A Free Radio Handbook*

ROY SAN FILIPPO—*New World In Our Hearts: 8 Years of Writings from the Love and Rage Revolutionary Anarchist Federation, A*

ALEXANDRE SKIRDA—*Facing the Enemy: A History Of Anarchist Organisation From Proudhon To May 1968*

ALEXANDRE SKIRDA—*Nestor Mahkno—Anarchy's Cossack*

VALERIE SOLANAS—*Scum Manifesto*

CJ STONE—*Housing Benefit Hill & Other Places*

ANTONIO TELLEZ—*Sabate: Guerilla Extraordinary*

MICHAEL TOBIAS—*Rage and Reason*

JIM TULLY—*Beggars of Life: A Hobo Autobiography*

TOM VAGUE—*Anarchy in the UK: The Angry Brigade*

TOM VAGUE—*Great British Mistake, The*

TOM VAGUE—*Televisionaries*

JAN VALTIN—*Out of the Night*

RAOUL VANEIGEM—*Cavalier History Of Surrealism, A*

FRANCOIS EUGENE VIDOCQ—*Memoirs of Vidocq: Master of Crime*

GEE VOUCHER—*Crass Art And Other Pre-Postmodern Monsters*

MARK J WHITE—*Idol Killing, An*

JOHN YATES—*Controlled Flight Into Terrain*

JOHN YATES—*September Commando*

BENJAMIN ZEPHANIAH—*Little Book of Vegan Poems*

BENJAMIN ZEPHANIAH—*School's Out*

HELLO—*2/15: The Day The World Said NO To War*

DARK STAR COLLECTIVE —*Beneath the Paving Stones: Situationists and the Beach, May 68*

DARK STAR COLLECTIVE —*Quiet Rumours: An Anarcha-Feminist Reader*

ANONYMOUS —*Test Card F*

CLASS WAR FEDERATION —*Unfinished Business: The Politics of Class War*

CDs

THE EX—*1936: The Spanish Revolution*

MUMIA ABU JAMAL—*175 Progress Drive*

MUMIA ABU JAMAL—*All Things Censored Vol. 1*

MUMIA ABU JAMAL—*Spoken Word*

FREEDOM ARCHIVES—*Chile: Promise of Freedom*

FREEDOM ARCHIVES—*Prisons on Fire: George Jackson, Attica & Black Liberation*

JUDI BARI—*Who Bombed Judi Bari?*

JELLO BIAFRA—*Become the Media*

JELLO BIAFRA—*Beyond The Valley of the Gift Police*

JELLO BIAFRA—*High Priest of Harmful*

JELLO BIAFRA—*I Blow Minds For A Living*

JELLO BIAFRA—*If Evolution Is Outlawed*

JELLO BIAFRA—*Machine Gun In The Clown's Hand*

JELLO BIAFRA—*No More Cocoons*

NOAM CHOMSKY—*American Addiction, An*

NOAM CHOMSKY—*Case Studies in Hypocrisy*

NOAM CHOMSKY—*Emerging Framework of World Power*

NOAM CHOMSKY—*Free Market Fantasies*

NOAM CHOMSKY—*New War On Terrorism: Fact And Fiction*

NOAM CHOMSKY—*Propaganda and Control of the Public Mind*

NOAM CHOMSKY—*Prospects for Democracy*

NOAM CHOMSKY/CHUMBAWAMBA—*For A Free Humanity: For Anarchy*

WARD CHURCHILL—*Doing Time: The Politics of Imprisonment*

WARD CHURCHILL—*In A Pig's Eye: Reflections on the Police State, Repression, and Native America*

WARD CHURCHILL—*Life in Occupied America*

WARD CHURCHILL—*Pacifism and Pathology in the American Left*

ALEXANDER COCKBURN—*Beating the Devil: The Incendiary Rants of Alexander Cockburn*

ANGELA DAVIS—*Prison Industrial Complex, The*

JAMES KELMAN—*Seven Stories*

TOM LEONARD—*Nora's Place and Other Poems 1965–99*

CHRISTIAN PARENTI—*Taking Liberties: Policing, Prisons and Surveillance in an Age of Crisis*

UTAH PHILLIPS—*I've Got To know*

DAVID ROVICS—*Behind the Barricades: Best of David Rovics*

ARUNDHATI ROY—*Come September*

VARIOUS—*Better Read Than Dead*

VARIOUS—*Less Rock, More Talk*

VARIOUS—*Mob Action Against the State: Collected Speeches from the Bay Area Anarchist Bookfair*

VARIOUS—*Monkeywrenching the New World Order*

VARIOUS—*Return of the Read Menace*

HOWARD ZINN—*Artists In A Time of War*

HOWARD ZINN—*Heroes and Martyrs: Emma Goldman, Sacco & Vanzetti, and the Revolutionary Struggle*

HOWARD ZINN—*People's History of the United States: A Lecture at Reed College, A*

HOWARD ZINN—*People's History Project*

HOWARD ZINN–*Stories Hollywood Never Tells*

DVDs

NOAM CHOMSKY—*Distorted Morality*

ARUNDHATI ROY—*Instant Mix Imperial Democracy*

Printed in the USA
CPSIA information can be obtained
at www.ICGtesting.com
JSHW060045150824
68134JS00031B/2634